Front Matter

This book is dedicated to the brave men and women of the fire service, the selfless individuals who risk their lives daily to protect our communities. It is a testament to their unwavering courage, dedication, and unwavering commitment to service. This work is also dedicated to the instructors and training officers who tirelessly pour their knowledge, experience, and passion into shaping the next generation of firefighters. Your dedication to excellence in training is the bedrock upon which the safety and success of our fire services are built. You are the unsung heroes who cultivate the skills, knowledge, and resilience necessary to face the ever-evolving challenges of this demanding profession. Your impact extends far beyond the classroom, shaping not only the careers of individual firefighters, but also the very fabric of community safety. Thank you for your unwavering commitment to excellence and for your service to humanity. To the families who support these brave individuals, your sacrifices and unwavering support are invaluable, enabling our firefighters to focus on their critical mission. This book is a small token of appreciation for your significant contribution.

The fire service is a profession built on tradition, a testament to time-honored practices passed down through generations of courageous firefighters. Yet, the world around us is rapidly changing. Our recruits—shaped by a digital age and the unprecedented disruptions of the COVID-19 pandemic—bring with them unique learning styles and experiences. This book challenges us to bridge the gap between established methods and the needs of a modern learning environment. "Why Before the How" is not about abandoning the proven techniques that underpin our profession's success; rather, it's a call for a mindful evolution in our approach to recruit training. It's about recognizing the importance of fostering genuine understanding, not just rote memorization, and building a foundation of "why" that empowers recruits to truly master the "how." We must prioritize meaningful engagement, replacing outdated lectures with active learning methodologies and fostering a passion for the profession that extends far beyond the completion of training. This book offers practical strategies to achieve this. It's a testament to the significant investment departments make in their firefighters, highlighting how effective training—a training that truly connects with our recruits—delivers an exceptional return. It's a roadmap to creating a training experience that is not only effective but inspiring, preparing a new generation of firefighters ready to meet the complex challenges of the future.

For decades, fire service recruit training has often relied on traditional, lecture-based methodologies, sometimes referred to as "death by PowerPoint." While these methods have served their purpose, they often fall short in engaging today's recruits. The digital age and the recent experiences of the COVID-19 pandemic have fundamentally altered how younger generations learn and process information. Modern recruits, accustomed to interactive online learning and self-directed education, respond less effectively to passive learning models. This book introduces a revolutionary approach: "Why Before the How." This pedagogical shift prioritizes understanding the underlying rationale and significance of each firefighting technique before delving into the specific procedural steps. By emphasizing the "why," we foster deeper comprehension, enhanced retention, and ultimately, improved performance. We move beyond simply instructing recruits on "how" to perform tasks, and instead, we equip them with a comprehensive understanding of the principles and context that drive these actions. This results in a more engaged and motivated recruit who possesses a stronger foundation and a greater appreciation for the profession. This book not only explains the philosophy behind "Why Before the How," but also provides practical, evidence-based strategies for implementation. It offers detailed examples, case studies, and actionable advice, enabling training officers to seamlessly integrate these techniques into their existing training programs. We will explore various methods to improve engagement, addressing the challenges of diverse learning styles, limited resources, and the importance of ongoing assessment. Ultimately, this book aims to empower instructors to cultivate a lifelong love of learning and commitment to continuous professional development within the recruits, shaping them into well-rounded, highly competent, and dedicated firefighters who are prepared for the ever-evolving challenges of the modern fire service.

Chapter 1: The Evolving Landscape of Fire Service Recruit Training

The landscape of fire service recruit training is undergoing a significant transformation, driven largely by the changing demographics of the recruits themselves. Gone are the days when recruits primarily consisted of young men straight out of high school, possessing a limited exposure to technology and largely relying on traditional, instructor-led learning. Today's recruits represent a much broader spectrum of ages, backgrounds, and learning styles, profoundly impacting how training needs to be delivered.

This shift is most prominently seen in the prevalence of digital natives. These individuals have grown up immersed in technology, accustomed to self-directed online learning, and comfortable navigating the digital world. They are often accustomed to instant feedback, readily available information, and interactive learning experiences. This contrasts starkly with the previous generations of firefighters, who may have learned primarily through traditional lectures, rote memorization, and hands-on practice under the direct supervision of experienced mentors. This difference in learning styles necessitates a pedagogical shift to cater to the needs and preferences of today's recruits.

Furthermore, the educational backgrounds of recruits are increasingly diverse. While some still come directly from high school, many possess college degrees, vocational training, or prior work experience in related fields. This prior learning shapes their expectations and influences their learning approaches. A recruit with a background in paramedicine, for example, may already possess a strong understanding of emergency medical response principles, requiring a different level of instruction than a recruit with no prior healthcare experience. Similarly, recruits with prior military experience may exhibit a different learning style, potentially more comfortable with structured environments and hierarchical systems. Recognizing and adapting to these varied experiences is crucial for effective training.

Understanding various learning preferences is paramount. Some learners thrive in visual learning environments, responding well to diagrams, videos, and demonstrations. Others prefer auditory learning, benefitting from lectures, discussions, and audio-based training materials. Kinesthetic learners, on the other hand, require hands-on experience and physical practice to effectively grasp concepts. Modern training programs must incorporate diverse learning styles, utilizing a blend of teaching methodologies to cater to the strengths of each individual recruit. Ignoring these differences can lead to frustration, decreased engagement, and ultimately, lower retention rates.

The availability of readily accessible online resources also plays a significant role. Recruits can access a wealth of information online, often independently exploring topics of interest before formal training begins. This self-directed learning can be beneficial, expanding their knowledge base and providing them with a foundation upon which to build upon. However, it also presents a challenge. The information available online is not always accurate, reliable, or up-to-date with current fire service standards and procedures. Training officers must therefore guide recruits towards credible sources and ensure that they critically evaluate the information they encounter.

Beyond the technical aspects, the motivational factors influencing modern recruits differ too. Previous generations of firefighters might have been driven primarily by a sense of civic duty and tradition. Today's recruits are often influenced by a wider range of factors, including career prospects, personal growth, and the opportunity to make a tangible difference in their communities. Understanding these diverse motivations is essential for tailoring training programs that resonate with individual recruits. Incorporating elements of leadership training, self-improvement workshops, and community engagement into the overall training curriculum could enhance both engagement and motivation.

The impact of societal shifts on recruits' expectations cannot be ignored. Increased awareness of mental health and well-being, for instance, necessitates a more supportive and understanding training environment. Recruits may expect open communication channels, access to mental health resources, and a training culture that prioritizes their physical and emotional well-being. The traditional hierarchical structure of the fire service is also being challenged. Recruits often prefer a collaborative, less authoritarian learning environment where their input is valued and their questions are encouraged. A shift towards participatory learning, involving recruits in the design and delivery of training exercises, can contribute to a more positive and engaging experience.

Moreover, the increasing diversity of recruits in terms of race, ethnicity, gender, and sexual orientation necessitates an inclusive training environment. Training materials should reflect this diversity, showcasing a broad range of role models and avoiding stereotypes. Training exercises should simulate realistic scenarios encountered in diverse communities, ensuring that recruits are prepared to effectively serve all members of society. The training environment itself should be free of bias, discrimination, and harassment, fostering a sense of belonging and encouraging participation from all recruits.

Addressing the learning styles and expectations of modern recruits requires a proactive and innovative approach to training. Simply replicating the traditional methods of the past will not suffice. Fire service training officers need to embrace modern pedagogical approaches, incorporating technology, diverse learning strategies, and inclusive practices. This approach not only enhances recruit engagement and knowledge retention but also ultimately improves public safety by ensuring that firefighters are well-prepared and equipped to face the challenges of a modern world.

Furthermore, understanding the changing demographics of recruits is not simply about adapting to a new generation. It is about recognizing that a diverse and inclusive fire service is a stronger and more effective fire service. By embracing the varied skills, experiences, and perspectives of a diverse pool of recruits, fire departments can enhance their overall capacity to serve their communities and meet the increasingly complex demands of modern firefighting. This shift requires a commitment to creating a truly inclusive training environment, where all recruits feel valued, respected, and empowered to reach their full potential.

The need to adapt training is not solely about accommodating individual learning styles but also ensuring the development of well-rounded, resilient firefighters. This includes incorporating training modules on mental health, stress management, and resilience, recognizing that these aspects are crucial for career longevity and overall well-being. The financial investment in recruit training is substantial, making it imperative that training departments focus on strategies to optimize return on investment (ROI). The financial cost of ineffective training, measured in terms of increased incident response times, higher injury rates, lower morale, and increased turnover, far outweighs the initial investment in developing efficient and engaging training programs.

Finally, training officers themselves require ongoing professional development. They must adapt their teaching methods, staying abreast of the latest pedagogical approaches and incorporating technological advancements. Professional development opportunities, including workshops, conferences, and access to relevant online resources, are vital to ensure that instructors remain equipped to train the next generation of firefighters effectively. The ongoing evolution of the fire service demands that training officers remain committed to continuous learning, ensuring that their teaching methodologies are constantly refined and updated. In conclusion, understanding and accommodating the changing demographics of fire service recruits is not merely an adaptation but a strategic necessity for enhancing the effectiveness, diversity, and resilience of the fire service.

The onset of the COVID-19 pandemic in 2020 presented an unprecedented challenge to fire service recruit training programs worldwide. The sudden implementation of social distancing measures, lockdowns, and restrictions on group gatherings forced training officers to rapidly adapt their methods, often with limited resources and time. Traditional training methodologies, heavily reliant on hands-on exercises, close-quarters simulations, and in-person lectures, were rendered largely impossible overnight. This disruption exposed vulnerabilities in the existing training infrastructure and necessitated a radical re-evaluation of established practices.

One of the most immediate impacts was the suspension of in-person classroom instruction. Lectures, previously a cornerstone of fire service training, were abruptly replaced by online alternatives. This transition, while necessary, presented significant challenges. The effectiveness of online lectures in conveying complex technical information, particularly the nuances of firefighting tactics and strategic decision-making, was immediately questioned. The lack of immediate feedback and the potential for distractions in a home learning environment raised concerns about knowledge retention and practical skills development. Many training officers, accustomed to the immediacy of in-person interaction, struggled to adapt to the limitations and asynchronous nature of online learning platforms.

Furthermore, the practical components of fire service training, arguably the most crucial aspect of the curriculum, were severely impacted. Hands-on exercises involving simulated fires, confined space rescue scenarios, and high-rise evacuations became highly problematic due to social distancing restrictions. The reliance on close physical contact and collaborative teamwork, fundamental elements of firefighting, were largely incompatible with the need to maintain a safe physical distance. This led to a significant decrease in the amount of practical training that could be delivered, raising concerns about the preparedness of new recruits. Innovative solutions, such as scaled-down simulations, socially distanced training drills, and the use of virtual reality (VR) technology, were explored but often faced limitations in terms of accessibility and effectiveness.

The limitations imposed by the pandemic also extended beyond the practical aspects of training. The assessment of recruits' skills and knowledge was also significantly affected. Traditional methods of assessment, involving observation of recruits' performance during hands-on exercises and written examinations conducted in a controlled environment, became difficult to implement. This necessitated the development of alternative assessment methods, such as online quizzes, remote simulations, and video submissions of practical skills demonstrations. While these methods offered a degree of flexibility, they also raised concerns about the objectivity and fairness of the assessment process and the difficulty of accurately evaluating practical proficiency remotely. The need for robust and reliable remote assessment methods became a high priority, demanding innovative solutions and careful calibration.

However, the pandemic's impact was not entirely negative. The need for rapid adaptation spurred innovation and creativity within the fire service training community. The widespread adoption of online learning platforms, while initially challenging, ultimately facilitated access to a wider range of training resources and a greater degree of flexibility in training delivery. The development of online modules and interactive simulations allowed recruits to access training materials at their own pace and revisit complex concepts as needed. This personalized learning approach, while not replacing entirely the value of hands-on training, proved to be a valuable supplement to traditional methods.

The pandemic accelerated the adoption of technology in fire service training. Virtual reality (VR) and augmented reality (AR) technologies, previously explored but not widely implemented, gained significant traction as tools for simulating real-world scenarios without the risks associated with physical interaction. These technologies allowed recruits to experience immersive training environments, practice critical decision-making under pressure, and improve their situational awareness in a safe and controlled setting. The use of VR and AR also offered cost-effective solutions by reducing the need for expensive and potentially hazardous training facilities. The pandemic's forced experimentation with these new technologies laid the foundation for their broader adoption in future training programs, even after the immediate threat of the pandemic receded.

The crisis also highlighted the importance of robust communication and collaboration. Training officers needed to maintain consistent communication with recruits, providing clear guidance, support, and regular updates on training schedules and procedures. Furthermore, collaboration between training departments and organizations across geographical boundaries became crucial for sharing best practices, innovative solutions, and resources. The pandemic fostered a sense of shared responsibility and collective problem-solving, strengthening professional networks and promoting a more unified approach to fire service training.

The pandemic-induced changes also extended to the assessment of training effectiveness. The traditional methods of evaluating training outcomes, often focused on pass/fail rates and test scores, were insufficient in capturing the impact of the disruption caused by the pandemic. More nuanced evaluation methods were needed to assess the effectiveness of remote learning, the impact of reduced hands-on training, and the overall preparedness of recruits entering the field. This led to a greater emphasis on collecting data, tracking individual recruit progress, and conducting feedback sessions to evaluate the efficacy of new training approaches. This focus on data-driven evaluation allowed for continuous improvement and adaptation of training programs to better meet the needs of recruits and the demands of the profession.

The experience of navigating the COVID-19 pandemic provided invaluable lessons for fire service training officers. It underscored the need for adaptability, resilience, and the willingness to embrace innovative technologies and pedagogical approaches. The pandemic acted as a catalyst, accelerating the adoption of online learning, VR/AR technologies, and remote assessment methods, ultimately enriching and diversifying the range of training tools available to fire service departments. The insights gained from this period of disruption will continue to shape the evolution of fire service recruit training in the years to come, ensuring that the training programs are more resilient, accessible, and effectively prepare future firefighters for the challenges of a constantly evolving world. The investment in robust, adaptable, and technology-enabled training is no longer optional; it's essential for the safety of the public and the well-being of our firefighters. The lessons learned during the pandemic should not be forgotten but rather utilized to improve and refine training methodologies for the long-term. The shift towards a more blended learning approach, combining online and in-person instruction, should be embraced to cater to diverse learning styles and ensure greater engagement and knowledge retention. The enhanced focus on data-driven decision making in training should persist, ensuring ongoing refinement and continuous improvement. The emphasis on robust communication and collaboration, strengthened by the pandemic, must remain a key element in delivering effective training programs. In conclusion, the COVID-19 pandemic forced a re-evaluation of traditional fire service training, sparking innovation and leading to lasting improvements in training methodologies. The adaptive strategies adopted during this challenging period will serve as a blueprint for future training programs, contributing to a safer and more effective fire service.

The limitations of traditional fire service recruit training methods are starkly apparent when considering the learning styles and expectations of today's recruits. For decades, the dominant paradigm has been the "death by PowerPoint" approach: lengthy lectures filled with dense information, often delivered in a monotone voice, with minimal opportunities for interaction or hands-on application. This method, while perhaps functional in a bygone era, fails to resonate with modern learners who have grown up in a world saturated with readily accessible information and engaging multimedia content. The passive nature of this approach leads to poor knowledge retention and a disengaged learning environment. Recruits, accustomed to interactive online learning and self-directed study, find this style tedious and ineffective.

The inherent problem with the lecture-heavy model lies in its failure to cater to diverse learning styles. While some recruits may benefit from absorbing information auditorily, many others require visual aids, kinesthetic activities, or collaborative learning experiences to truly grasp complex concepts. The "one-size-fits-all" approach of traditional training fails to acknowledge this inherent diversity, resulting in uneven learning outcomes and potential frustration among those who don't learn effectively through passive listening. For instance, explaining the intricacies of a hydraulic rescue system solely through a lecture can be vastly less effective than allowing recruits to physically manipulate the equipment, work through simulations, and troubleshoot potential problems. The practical application solidifies the theoretical knowledge and fosters a deeper understanding of the system's mechanics.

Furthermore, the traditional model often suffers from a lack of contextualization. Simply presenting facts and procedures without explaining the underlying rationale or the "why" behind them leaves recruits feeling disconnected and unmotivated. They may memorize steps for a particular operation, but lack a true understanding of its significance and potential consequences. For example, teaching the proper procedure for donning personal protective equipment (PPE) without explaining the specific risks associated with each piece of equipment (e.g., the importance of thermal protection, the vulnerability of exposed skin, the mechanics of proper SCBA usage) fails to impart the critical life-saving reasoning behind the procedure. This approach limits the capacity for critical thinking and problem-solving, crucial skills for effective firefighting.

The issue of knowledge retention is another critical limitation of traditional methods. Passive listening leads to a decline in long-term memory and recall. Recruits may appear to understand the material during the initial lecture, but their ability to apply this knowledge in real-world situations diminishes rapidly without reinforcement and practical application. This is especially concerning in a high-stakes environment like firefighting where split-second decisions and precise actions are paramount. To counter this, training methodologies must incorporate regular opportunities for recall, review, and practice, moving away from one-off lectures and instead adopting spaced repetition techniques, knowledge checks and regular refresher courses. Interactive simulations, scenario-based training, and practical exercises serve as crucial tools for enhancing knowledge retention and skills development.

Moreover, the traditional approach often neglects the crucial role of feedback and formative assessment. In a lecture-style environment, instructors rarely receive immediate insights into individual recruit understanding, limiting their ability to address misconceptions or tailor their instruction to specific learning needs. Constructive feedback is vital for skill development and allows for a more dynamic and responsive learning experience. Incorporating regular quizzes, practical demonstrations, and peer reviews provides opportunities for instructors to gauge comprehension, identify areas needing improvement, and provide tailored support. This proactive feedback mechanism enhances learning, promotes self-awareness, and fosters a culture of continuous improvement.

The lack of engagement is another significant drawback. Traditional training methodologies often fail to capture and maintain recruits' attention, leading to boredom, disinterest, and ultimately, reduced learning outcomes. The passive nature of lectures can be especially detrimental in a field that requires constant alertness, rapid decision-making, and acute situational awareness. Firefighting recruits need to be actively involved in their training, not simply passive recipients of information. Incorporating active learning strategies, such as group discussions, case studies, simulations, and role-playing, significantly improves engagement and motivation.

Furthermore, the traditional training model often overlooks the importance of fostering a positive learning environment. A stressful, competitive, or punitive atmosphere can hinder learning and diminish recruits' overall experience. Fire service instructors hold a significant role in shaping the attitudes and perceptions of future firefighters. Cultivating a supportive and encouraging environment, emphasizing teamwork and collaboration, and celebrating achievements will promote confidence, build camaraderie, and encourage a lifelong commitment to the profession. This includes actively seeking and incorporating recruits' feedback into the training process and recognizing their unique learning styles and needs.

The effectiveness of traditional fire service training methods is further compromised by its rigidity. The emphasis on standardized procedures and techniques, while crucial for safety and consistency, can stifle creativity and adaptability. Firefighting is a dynamic profession, and recruits need to be equipped with the critical thinking skills and problem-solving abilities to handle unexpected situations and emergencies. Rigid adherence to pre-determined protocols can limit their capacity to think critically, assess risks, and make informed decisions under pressure. Training must integrate scenarios that necessitate improvisation, collaboration, and creative problem-solving.

This is best achieved through the implementation of realistic simulations and scenario-based training.

Finally, the lack of integration between theory and practice is a recurring challenge in traditional training. The disconnect between classroom learning and practical application can lead to a fragmented learning experience and an inability to transfer knowledge into real-world contexts. The compartmentalization of training elements hinders the development of holistic understanding and fails to prepare recruits for the complexity of firefighting operations. Effective training must seamlessly integrate theoretical knowledge with hands-on practice, providing recruits with multiple opportunities to apply their learning in simulated and realistic environments.

In summary, traditional "death by PowerPoint" methods, while once standard, fall short in meeting the needs and learning preferences of contemporary recruits. The lack of engagement, inadequate knowledge retention, insufficient feedback mechanisms, absence of contextualization, rigid approach and limited integration of theory and practice severely limit the effectiveness of such training. The evolving landscape of fire service demands a more holistic and dynamic approach to recruit training that emphasizes active learning, personalized instruction, and practical application. The next section will explore how modern pedagogical approaches can overcome these limitations and create a more engaging, effective, and rewarding training experience.

The financial implications of inadequate fire service training are substantial and often overlooked. Departments invest heavily in recruiting, equipping, and training their personnel. This investment represents a significant portion of a fire department's overall budget, encompassing salaries, benefits, training materials, equipment, and facilities. When training is ineffective, this investment yields a drastically reduced return. Poorly trained firefighters are more likely to make critical errors, increasing the risk of injury or fatality to themselves and the public they serve. These incidents result in direct costs associated with medical care, workers' compensation claims, legal settlements, and equipment damage. Furthermore, ineffective training can lead to inefficient operations, longer response times, and increased property damage, further escalating the financial burden.

Consider the cost of a single serious injury or fatality. The direct medical expenses, lost wages, and potential legal ramifications can quickly reach into the millions of dollars. These costs are not limited to the individual firefighter; they extend to the department, the municipality, and potentially even the insurance provider. The indirect costs are equally significant. Investigative reports, internal reviews, and the need to retrain personnel all add to the financial strain. The reputational damage stemming from such incidents can also lead to decreased public trust and support for the fire service, potentially impacting future funding and recruitment efforts.

Conversely, effective training demonstrably minimizes these risks. Well-trained firefighters are better equipped to handle emergencies safely and efficiently. This translates into a significant reduction in injuries, fatalities, and property damage. Improved operational efficiency, faster response times, and enhanced public safety are all direct outcomes of a robust training program. Data from various sources consistently demonstrates a strong correlation between effective training programs and improved performance metrics. Studies analyzing firefighter injury rates, for instance, have shown a significant reduction in injuries in departments that have implemented modern, engaging training methods. This is not just anecdotal evidence; it's backed up by quantifiable data.

Beyond the immediate cost avoidance, effective training fosters a culture of safety and continuous improvement within the department. Firefighters who feel adequately trained and supported are more likely to embrace safe practices and proactively identify potential hazards. This proactive approach minimizes the risk of accidents and incidents, further reducing costs in the long run. Furthermore, a well-trained workforce enhances morale and job satisfaction, leading to increased retention rates and reduced recruitment costs. The cost of replacing experienced personnel significantly exceeds the cost of investing in their ongoing professional development.

The return on investment (ROI) of effective training extends beyond the immediate financial benefits. It also encompasses intangible but equally important factors like public trust and confidence. A department with a reputation for excellence in training and a commitment to public safety garners more support from the community and its governing bodies. This translates into increased funding opportunities and a stronger overall position within the community. Effective training is a long-term investment, fostering a culture of professionalism, safety, and efficiency that yields benefits for years to come.

The argument for a substantial investment in modern, effective fire service training rests on solid, data-driven foundations. Numerous studies correlate robust training programs with significantly reduced incident rates, fewer injuries, and lower property damage. For example, a study conducted by the National Fire Protection Association (NFPA) showed a marked decrease in firefighter injuries in departments that implemented comprehensive, hands-on training programs. These programs emphasized practical skills, scenario-based training, and the integration of advanced simulation techniques. The study also highlighted the positive impact of these training programs on firefighter morale and job satisfaction, leading to increased retention rates.

Furthermore, independent research has explored the economic impact of firefighter injuries. These analyses demonstrate the significant costs associated with medical care, lost wages, and legal liabilities. The financial burden extends beyond the injured firefighter, impacting the department, the municipality, and potentially the insurance providers. The economic analysis clearly demonstrates the substantial savings achieved through the prevention of such incidents, thereby underscoring the importance of effective, proactive training.

It's crucial to consider the holistic nature of ROI when assessing the effectiveness of fire service training. It's not merely about reducing costs, but also about enhancing performance, increasing safety, and promoting a positive working environment. A well-trained firefighter is a more confident firefighter, leading to improved response times and more effective interventions. This confidence stems not only from acquired skills but also from the understanding of the rationale behind techniques and procedures, the 'why' as well as the 'how,' an approach championed throughout this book.

Furthermore, effective training fosters a culture of continuous improvement and learning within the fire service. Firefighters who are continuously learning and developing their skills are better prepared to handle the evolving challenges faced by modern fire departments. This culture of continuous learning reduces the likelihood of complacency and promotes a proactive approach to safety. The long-term benefits of this proactive approach are significant, resulting in a safer and more efficient fire service.

Effective training also significantly impacts firefighter morale and job satisfaction. Firefighters who feel well-prepared and supported are more likely to be engaged and committed to their work. This heightened morale translates into a more efficient and productive workforce. The positive impact on morale also reduces turnover, which significantly reduces recruitment and training costs associated with replacing experienced personnel.

The integration of technology, such as virtual reality and augmented reality simulations, is revolutionizing fire service training. These tools offer realistic and immersive training experiences that provide recruits with opportunities to practice essential skills in a safe and controlled environment. The cost savings associated with using these technologies outweigh the initial investment in the long run due to reductions in injuries and property damage. The use of such technology improves learning outcomes, enhances knowledge retention, and significantly reduces the reliance on costly live-fire training exercises.

In conclusion, the ROI of effective fire service training is multifaceted and substantial. It encompasses not only the direct cost savings associated with reduced injuries and incidents but also the intangible benefits of enhanced public trust, improved firefighter morale, and the development of a culture of continuous learning. A strong commitment to effective training is not simply a prudent financial decision, but an investment in the safety, efficiency, and future of the fire service. The financial argument for modern, engaging training methods, which emphasize active learning and a deeper understanding of the 'why' behind procedures, is overwhelming and undeniably significant. The costs of inadequate training far exceed the investment required to create and maintain a high-quality, effective program. This investment is not merely a budgetary item; it's an investment in lives and the safety of the communities these professionals serve.

The modern fire service operates in an environment of escalating complexity. No longer are we solely dealing with straightforward structure fires; we face a myriad of challenges, from hazardous materials incidents and high-rise blazes to complex rescue operations and increasingly sophisticated technological threats. Our recruits, the future of the fire service, need a training regimen that equips them not just with the skills, but with the deep understanding necessary to navigate these multifaceted emergencies effectively and safely. This is where the "Why Before the How" philosophy becomes paramount.

Traditional training methods often fall into the trap of focusing primarily on the "how" – the mechanics of a particular technique or procedure. Recruits are shown how to operate a chainsaw, how to deploy a ladder, how to use a hoseline. While these skills are undoubtedly essential, without a thorough understanding of the *why* behind these actions, their application becomes rote, potentially leading to errors in judgment under the pressure of a real emergency. Imagine a recruit flawlessly executing a ladder raise, but failing to assess the wind conditions or the structural integrity of the building. The "how" is mastered, but the "why" – the critical thinking, the risk assessment – is missing.

This book advocates for a radical shift in our approach. We propose inverting the traditional model. Instead of starting with the "how," we begin with the "why." We start by fostering a comprehensive understanding of the underlying principles, the scientific basis, and the strategic rationale behind every firefighting technique. Why do we use a specific knot? Why is a particular ventilation technique preferred? Why is scene safety paramount before even considering extinguishing the fire?

This isn't simply about adding a theoretical layer to practical training; it's about fundamentally restructuring the learning process to enhance comprehension, retention, and ultimately, performance. When recruits understand the rationale behind a procedure, they develop a more profound understanding of its purpose and limitations. This understanding transforms a mere skill into a tool they can adapt and apply intelligently in diverse and unexpected situations. A firefighter who understands the principles of thermal layering will instinctively know how to better protect themselves and their crew during a structure fire. They will be less likely to take shortcuts or make impulsive decisions that could compromise safety.

The benefits of this approach extend beyond improved skill acquisition. By prioritizing the "why," we nurture a culture of critical thinking and problem-solving within the recruit class. We instill a mindset that prioritizes safety, risk assessment, and effective teamwork, building a foundation for a long and successful career. This is particularly important in the context of the ever-evolving challenges faced by the modern fire service. New technologies, new materials, and new threats demand adaptability and a willingness to learn and adapt. This mindset is not taught solely through demonstration but cultivated through an environment of inquiry.

The "Why Before the How" methodology also addresses the changing learning styles of modern recruits. The digital age has fostered a generation of self-directed learners accustomed to accessing information online and through interactive platforms. The traditional lecture-style delivery often struggles to engage this demographic, leading to disengagement and decreased learning outcomes. By focusing on the underlying reasons, by encouraging questions and discussion, and by using interactive techniques, we tailor our training to meet their learning preferences. We transform the learning environment from a passive experience to an active and engaging one, leading to improved knowledge retention and ultimately, better prepared firefighters.

The COVID-19 pandemic further highlighted the need for adaptable training methods. The limitations imposed by lockdowns and social distancing necessitated the adoption of new technologies and remote learning strategies. The "Why Before the How" philosophy lends itself naturally to these changes. Online learning platforms, interactive simulations, and virtual reality training can all be employed to effectively deliver the underlying principles of firefighting techniques. These technologies allow for flexible and individualized learning, catering to the needs of each recruit, regardless of location or circumstance.

Investing in this approach is not just about improving training outcomes; it's about investing in the future of the fire service. It's a financial investment that yields significant returns. We've already touched upon the economic consequences of inadequate training. Now, let's examine how the "Why Before the How" approach mitigates those risks and strengthens the department's overall performance.

The cost of training, while significant, pales in comparison to the costs associated with preventable injuries, fatalities, or property damage. By fostering a deeper understanding of the "why," we significantly reduce the probability of errors in judgment. Recruits who understand the rationale behind their actions are less prone to making mistakes that could have serious consequences. This translates to fewer injuries, reduced equipment damage, and lower legal and insurance costs. This cost-benefit analysis clearly demonstrates that prioritizing the "why" is a fiscally responsible approach.

Furthermore, the improved competence fostered by this approach translates to increased efficiency and effectiveness. Firefighters who thoroughly grasp the principles of their profession are better equipped to handle emergencies swiftly and safely. This enhanced performance can lead to reduced response times, minimized property damage, and improved public safety, indirectly generating cost savings through prevention. These positive outcomes strengthen community trust and enhance the overall reputation of the department.

Beyond the immediate financial benefits, the "Why Before the How" philosophy fosters a culture of continuous learning and professional development. Firefighters who understand the underlying principles are more likely to seek out further knowledge and embrace new technologies. They become lifelong learners, constantly seeking to improve their skills and adapt to the ever-changing demands of the profession. This ongoing professional development is vital in a field characterized by constant advancements and new challenges. This continuous improvement loop significantly reduces the need for extensive retraining later in a firefighter's career, further improving efficiency and cost-effectiveness.

Moreover, a training program that prioritizes comprehension and engagement enhances morale and job satisfaction. When recruits feel adequately prepared and understand the "why" behind their actions, their confidence increases. This, in turn, translates into a more positive and productive work environment. This increased morale leads to higher retention rates, reducing the costly cycle of recruiting and training new personnel. The long-term cost savings from reduced turnover are considerable, justifying the initial investment in this superior training methodology.

Finally, embracing the "Why Before the How" approach is not simply a tactical shift in training methodology; it is a philosophical commitment to nurturing the next generation of fire service professionals. It is about creating thoughtful, engaged, and resourceful firefighters capable of confronting the multifaceted challenges of the 21st century and beyond. It's about fostering a culture of continuous learning, safety, and a deep understanding of the profession. It's about empowering firefighters with the knowledge and confidence to not only react effectively but also to proactively mitigate risks and make sound, informed decisions, every time. This investment in the "why," therefore, is an investment in the future of the fire service, its safety, its efficiency, and its overall success. It's an investment worth making, and one that will yield invaluable returns for years to come.

Chapter 2: Implementing the 'Why Before the How' Approach

The success of the "Why Before the How" approach hinges on effectively breaking down complex procedures into digestible components. This isn't simply about shortening lengthy explanations; it's about strategically dissecting the process to reveal the underlying logic and interconnectedness of each step. Think of it like peeling an onion, layer by layer, revealing the core understanding at the heart of each firefighting technique. This layered approach allows recruits to grasp the "why" before grappling with the "how," fostering a deeper, more intuitive understanding of the overall procedure.

One effective strategy is to utilize a "backward chaining" method. Instead of starting with the initial step and progressing linearly, begin with the desired outcome or final objective of the procedure. For example, consider the process of rescuing a victim from a burning building using a ladder. The final objective is the safe extraction of the victim. Working backward, we break down the process into sequential steps: removing the victim from the ladder, securing the victim on the ladder, safely descending the ladder with the victim, positioning the ladder correctly, and finally, assessing the situation and choosing the appropriate ladder type and placement.

Each of these steps then undergoes further decomposition. Consider "positioning the ladder correctly." This seemingly simple step can be broken down into several sub-components: assessing the building's structural integrity, identifying a safe and stable placement point, considering wind conditions, ensuring proper ladder angle, and checking for overhead obstructions. Each sub-component can be further analyzed, for example, assessing building integrity involves understanding the types of building materials, identifying potential weak points, and considering the potential impact of the fire on the structural strength. This detailed breakdown ensures that the recruit understands not only what to do, but also *why* each decision is crucial for the success and safety of the operation.

This backward chaining approach allows for a gradual build-up of knowledge, starting with the overarching goal and then working backward to the individual steps. This fosters a clear understanding of the purpose and importance of each action. It also facilitates the identification of critical decision points within the procedure, highlighting areas requiring particular attention and training. Recruits can more easily visualize the consequences of errors at each stage, strengthening their commitment to safety and precision.

Another invaluable tool is the creation of visual aids. Flowcharts, diagrams, and even simple illustrations can greatly improve understanding. A flowchart can visually represent the sequential steps of a procedure, clearly indicating decision points and branching pathways. Diagrams can illustrate the spatial relationships and interactions between different elements of a procedure. For example, a diagram showing the appropriate placement and angle of a ladder relative to the building can reinforce understanding and eliminate ambiguity. Illustrations can simplify complex concepts, providing a visual representation of the underlying principles. For instance, an illustration depicting the thermal layering of a fire can significantly improve understanding of fire behavior and the importance of proper protective gear.

Beyond visual aids, incorporating interactive exercises and simulations can transform the learning process. Interactive simulations, for instance, can immerse recruits in realistic scenarios, allowing them to practice decision-making under pressure in a safe environment. These simulations can incorporate various variables, such as weather conditions, building type, and victim characteristics, demanding adaptable problem-solving skills. This hands-on experience allows recruits to apply the knowledge gained from understanding the "why" of the procedures directly, reinforcing their understanding and promoting retention. The integration of such interactive learning greatly enhances the effectiveness of the "Why Before the How" approach.

Consider the seemingly simple procedure of tying a bowline knot. The traditional approach might simply show the physical steps of tying the knot. However, a "Why Before the How" approach would delve into the reasons why the bowline is preferred in specific situations. It would emphasize its non-slipping properties, its ease of untying even under load, and its applications in various rescue and rigging scenarios. By understanding the properties and applications of the knot, recruits will not only learn to tie it correctly but also recognize when it is the most appropriate knot to use in a given situation, making informed decisions based on a thorough understanding.

Similarly, the procedure for using a fire extinguisher can be enhanced by explaining the different classes of fires, the types of extinguishing agents used, and the specific methods of application for each class. Understanding the chemical reactions involved in fire suppression improves the understanding of why a particular technique is effective for a given type of fire. Recruits will not only learn the proper technique but also understand the underlying scientific principles, leading to more efficient and safer fire suppression.

The "Why Before the How" approach extends beyond technical procedures to encompass crucial aspects of fireground leadership and teamwork. For instance, instead of simply teaching the mechanics of incident command system (ICS), instructors can explain the underlying principles of effective communication, delegation of tasks, and resource management. By understanding the "why" of each element of ICS, recruits will be better equipped to apply its principles effectively in dynamic and stressful situations, leading to improved coordination and enhanced safety outcomes.

To further enhance the learning process, incorporating real-world case studies and post-incident analysis is essential. Analyzing actual fire incidents allows recruits to examine the successes and failures of different approaches, underscoring the practical implications of the "why" behind firefighting procedures. For instance, reviewing a fire where inadequate ventilation led to a flashover can powerfully illustrate the importance of proper ventilation techniques and their impact on overall safety and success. This reflection and analysis reinforces the learning process, and helps contextualize the importance of a thorough understanding.

Moreover, regularly scheduled reviews and assessments throughout the training program are critical for reinforcing the concepts learned. These reviews should not just focus on the "how" but equally on the "why," testing the recruits' understanding of the underlying principles and their ability to apply them to various scenarios. This continuous evaluation process identifies any gaps in understanding and allows for timely remediation, ensuring that all recruits possess a solid foundation in both the technical skills and the underlying rationale behind them. This is particularly crucial given the evolving nature of the fire service and the introduction of new techniques and technologies.

The integration of technology into the training process can further enhance the effectiveness of the "Why Before the How" approach. Interactive simulations, virtual reality training, and online learning platforms can provide immersive and engaging learning experiences. These technologies allow recruits to explore different scenarios and practice decision-making in a safe and controlled environment, reinforcing their understanding and enhancing retention. The use of technology also allows for personalized learning experiences, catering to different learning styles and paces, ensuring that all recruits develop a deep and comprehensive understanding.

Finally, fostering a culture of inquiry and critical thinking is paramount. Encouraging recruits to ask questions, challenge assumptions, and explore different approaches promotes a deeper level of understanding and engagement. Creating a learning environment where questioning is valued and encouraged fosters a mindset of continuous learning and critical analysis, essential for success in the demanding fire service profession. This emphasis on inquiry ensures that the recruits not only understand the "why" but can actively apply this knowledge to improve their own practices and enhance their understanding of the profession. This commitment to questioning and critical thinking fosters a culture of ongoing professional development, a characteristic of high-performing firefighters. By embracing this approach, fire service training departments can nurture the next generation of fire service professionals, preparing them for the complexities and challenges of the modern fire service. The investment in understanding the "why" is an investment in a safer, more effective, and more resilient fire service.

The power of storytelling in fire service training is often underestimated. We've discussed breaking down complex procedures, using backward chaining, and incorporating visual aids, but the human brain is wired to remember narratives. Transforming training materials into compelling stories can dramatically increase engagement and retention, leaving a lasting impact on recruits far beyond the rote memorization of technical procedures.

Think about it: we all remember childhood stories, fables, and even personal anecdotes better than lists of facts. This is because stories tap into our emotions and create a connection with the information. They provide context, making the material relatable and meaningful. In fire service training, storytelling can bring abstract concepts to life, making them more understandable and memorable.

Instead of simply explaining the steps involved in a building search, consider telling the story of a real-world incident where a seemingly minor detail—like the position of a piece of furniture—made the difference between life and death. Paint a vivid picture of the scene: the smoke-filled room, the sounds of crackling flames, the frantic search for a trapped victim. This narrative not only illustrates the importance of thorough searching but also adds emotional weight, making the lesson unforgettable.

Crafting effective narratives for fire service training requires careful consideration of the audience and the learning objectives. The stories should be relevant, authentic, and engaging, avoiding overly simplistic or melodramatic portrayals. Authenticity is key; recruits can often spot a fabricated story a mile away, and it can damage credibility. Whenever possible, use real-life examples, anonymized to protect confidentiality, of incidents or challenges faced by firefighters. This provides context and showcases the practical application of the techniques being taught.

Consider structuring the story around a central conflict or challenge. Perhaps the story is about overcoming a difficult situation during a rescue operation, making a crucial decision under pressure, or even the everyday challenges of teamwork and communication within a fire crew. This framework immediately captures attention and creates suspense, leading recruits to actively follow the narrative and learn from the outcome.

Stories should also highlight both successes and failures. Learning from mistakes is a crucial aspect of fire service training, and stories provide an excellent platform for discussing errors and near misses. A narrative about an incident where a seemingly insignificant oversight led to a serious consequence can powerfully illustrate the importance of meticulous attention to detail and the need for constant vigilance.

For instance, the story of a firefighter who made a critical mistake during a rescue, highlighting the consequences and how the error could have been avoided, can be a powerful lesson in situational awareness and decision-making. Similarly, a story highlighting effective teamwork during a complex incident can demonstrate the importance of communication and coordination, emphasizing the collaborative nature of the profession.

The use of visuals can greatly enhance the effectiveness of storytelling in fire service training. Photographs, videos, and even interactive simulations can bring the story to life, immersing recruits in the scenario and fostering empathy with the individuals involved. Imagine showing a video of a real fire scene, then analyzing the events in detail and illustrating the importance of specific techniques and safety procedures. This would drive home the lessons learned far more effectively than a simple lecture.

Furthermore, integrating storytelling into a broader pedagogical approach, like experiential learning, can further enhance its effectiveness. After presenting a narrative case study, for example, recruits could engage in a simulation that mimics the described scenario. This allows them to test their knowledge and develop problem-solving skills in a safe and controlled environment, applying the lessons learned from the story to a hands-on experience.

Storytelling isn't just about recounting past events; it's about creating a shared experience and fostering a sense of community within the training environment. By sharing their own experiences and anecdotes, instructors can connect with recruits on a personal level, building rapport and trust. This creates a more comfortable learning environment, where recruits feel empowered to ask questions and actively participate in the learning process.

Encourage recruits to share their own stories, too. Ask them to discuss challenges they have faced, successes they have celebrated, or near misses they have encountered. This fosters a culture of open communication and shared learning, creating a collaborative learning environment where everyone feels comfortable sharing their experiences and insights. This approach also helps bridge the gap between theoretical knowledge and practical application, highlighting the importance of critical thinking and problem-solving skills.

Moreover, integrating storytelling with other modern pedagogical approaches, such as gamification and microlearning, can enhance its impact. For example, a series of short, engaging videos could present a storyline that unfolds over time, with each video building upon the previous one. This approach keeps recruits engaged and motivates them to continue learning, while simultaneously reinforcing key concepts and lessons. Gamification elements, such as points, badges, and leaderboards, could further enhance engagement and motivate recruits to strive for mastery.

Remember, the goal isn't to replace traditional training methods with storytelling; rather, it's to enhance and complement them. By weaving compelling narratives into the training curriculum, instructors can transform complex information into engaging and memorable experiences, fostering a deeper understanding of the fire service profession and cultivating a passion for the work. This integrated approach ensures that recruits not only acquire the technical skills necessary for the job but also develop the critical thinking and problem-solving abilities essential for success in the dynamic and demanding world of firefighting. The result is a more engaged, more knowledgeable, and ultimately, a safer and more effective fire service. The judicious use of storytelling transforms abstract concepts into tangible realities, leaving a far more impactful learning experience than traditional didactic methods.

Building upon the power of narrative in fire service training, we now turn our attention to the critical role of hands-on learning and experiential exercises. While storytelling provides context and emotional engagement, practical application is the cornerstone of mastering firefighting techniques. Simply understanding *why* a procedure is important isn't enough; recruits need to experience *how* it works in a safe, controlled environment. This section emphasizes integrating active learning strategies to solidify understanding and build competence.

The shift towards active learning isn't just a pedagogical trend; it's a recognition of how people learn best. Passive learning, such as lengthy lectures or PowerPoint presentations, often leads to poor retention and limited skill development. Active learning, on the other hand, involves direct participation, problem-solving, and immediate feedback. This approach fosters deeper understanding, enhances critical thinking, and ultimately results in more competent and confident firefighters.

One effective approach is the use of simulations. These can range from simple exercises, such as practicing knot-tying or using various rescue tools, to complex scenarios involving simulated fires, building searches, and rescue operations. The key is to create realistic scenarios that challenge recruits to apply their knowledge and skills in a safe environment. Simulations aren't about creating perfect replicas of real-world emergencies; they are about providing opportunities to practice decision-making under pressure, refine techniques, and learn from mistakes without risking injury or property damage.

For instance, consider a simulation focused on building searches. Instead of simply lecturing on search patterns and techniques, set up a mock building—even a simplified one using readily available materials—and have recruits practice different search methods. Provide them with various scenarios, such as locating a victim in a smoke-filled room or navigating a maze-like structure. Include obstacles to enhance the challenge and encourage problem-solving. Debriefing sessions after each simulation are vital. These sessions offer an opportunity to analyze performance, identify areas for improvement, and reinforce lessons learned.

Another powerful active learning technique is the use of case studies. Presenting recruits with real-world incidents—anonymized to protect privacy, of course—provides a context for applying theoretical knowledge. Case studies can be presented in various formats, such as written descriptions, video recordings, or interactive simulations. The critical aspect is the debriefing that follows. Encourage recruits to analyze the events, identify the key decisions made, evaluate the effectiveness of the responses, and suggest alternative approaches. This process encourages critical thinking and problem-solving, enhancing their ability to handle real-world situations.

Furthermore, integrating technology into hands-on learning can significantly enhance the experience. Virtual reality (VR) and augmented reality (AR) simulations offer immersive training environments where recruits can practice skills in realistic, yet safe, conditions. VR can replicate the sights, sounds, and even the physical sensations of a real fire scene, allowing recruits to experience the intensity and pressure of a real emergency without the inherent risks. AR overlays digital information onto the real world, providing real-time feedback and guidance during training exercises.

For example, AR can be used during hose handling drills, providing recruits with real-time feedback on their technique and identifying areas for improvement. Similarly, VR can simulate building searches, allowing recruits to practice navigating smoke-filled environments and locating victims in a safe and controlled setting. These technologies offer a level of realism and engagement that traditional methods simply can't match, providing valuable opportunities for skill development and knowledge retention.

Beyond simulations and technology, the simple act of practicing fundamental skills repeatedly is crucial. This seemingly straightforward approach shouldn't be underestimated. Proficiency in basic skills like knot-tying, hose handling, and equipment use is essential for effective firefighting. These skills require repetitive practice to develop muscle memory and proficiency. Regular drills, focusing on both individual and team-based skills, are vital for building confidence and ensuring readiness.

Consider incorporating gamification into these drills. Gamification introduces elements of game design—such as points, badges, and leaderboards—to enhance engagement and motivation. A simple points system rewarding accuracy and speed during knot-tying drills can significantly increase participation and enthusiasm. Leaderboards fostering friendly competition can further drive motivation and improvement. This approach transforms repetitive practice into an engaging and motivating activity, making the learning process more enjoyable and effective.

Incorporating peer teaching and mentoring is another valuable technique. Allowing more experienced recruits to assist in training newer members fosters a collaborative learning environment. This not only benefits the newer recruits but also reinforces the knowledge and skills of the mentors. The process of explaining procedures to others helps solidify understanding and identify any knowledge gaps. This reciprocal learning environment boosts confidence and establishes a sense of camaraderie within the recruit class.

Experiential learning isn't solely confined to structured exercises; it extends to incorporating real-world experiences wherever possible. This could include attending live fire training exercises, observing experienced firefighters in action, or participating in community outreach programs. Exposure to real-world situations, under appropriate supervision, provides invaluable learning experiences. These experiences, combined with debriefing sessions, provide context and relevance, making the training more meaningful and effective. Learning from observation and real-world application is invaluable, creating a powerful learning experience.

The integration of hands-on learning and experiential exercises is not an alternative to lectures and presentations; rather, it's a vital complement. The 'why'—the underlying rationale and importance of procedures—laid out in previous chapters provides the foundational knowledge. Hands-on exercises, simulations, and real-world experiences provide the practical application, solidifying understanding and building competence. This balanced approach maximizes learning outcomes and prepares recruits for the challenges of the firefighting profession. The combination of theoretical knowledge and practical experience creates well-rounded, confident, and competent firefighters. By investing in effective and engaging training methods, fire departments ensure they are developing the best possible personnel, ready to face any challenge. The ultimate goal is to cultivate a passion for the profession and empower recruits to become highly skilled and dedicated firefighters. This holistic approach, encompassing both theoretical understanding and practical application, leads to a more effective and ultimately, a safer fire service.

Utilizing technology effectively isn't simply about adopting the latest gadgets; it's about strategically integrating tools that enhance the learning experience and align with our "why before the how" philosophy. The goal is to create a more engaging and effective training environment that resonates with today's recruits, who are accustomed to interactive and technology-rich learning experiences. We need to move beyond the limitations of traditional methods and embrace the potential of technology to foster deeper understanding and improved skill retention.

One powerful tool is the use of simulations, extending beyond the simple exercises mentioned previously. Consider, for example, the use of virtual reality (VR) in fireground training. VR headsets can immerse recruits in realistic simulated fire scenarios, allowing them to practice search and rescue techniques, hose deployment, and other critical skills in a safe and controlled environment. The experience is significantly more engaging than a lecture or even a traditional training exercise. Imagine a recruit navigating a smoke-filled building in a VR simulation, experiencing the disorientation, the intense heat, and the pressure of finding a victim. This level of immersion helps them develop vital decision-making skills and build confidence in their abilities far beyond what a static training environment can provide.

Furthermore, VR offers the potential for repeated practice without the associated costs and risks of real-world training. Recruits can make mistakes, learn from them, and refine their skills in a virtual setting without any real-world consequences. This iterative learning process is particularly valuable in scenarios involving hazardous materials or complex rescue operations, where mistakes can have serious consequences. The ability to repeat scenarios, varying the parameters each time, allows for more nuanced learning and the development of a broader range of problem-solving skills. This is also far more cost effective than repeatedly setting up large scale, real-world training exercises.

Augmented reality (AR) provides another avenue for technological enhancement. AR overlays digital information onto the real world, providing recruits with real-time feedback and guidance during training exercises. Imagine a recruit practicing hose handling techniques with an AR overlay providing immediate feedback on their grip, hose deployment speed, and nozzle control. This immediate, personalized feedback is far more effective than relying on an instructor's post-exercise critique. AR can also be integrated into building search training exercises, providing recruits with real-time information about the building's layout, the location of victims, and potential hazards.

Beyond VR and AR, interactive learning platforms offer a versatile tool for enhancing engagement and knowledge retention. These platforms can incorporate a variety of learning modalities, including videos, quizzes, interactive simulations, and gamified challenges. They allow for self-paced learning, catering to individual learning styles and preferences. This flexibility is crucial in a diverse recruit class, ensuring that all recruits receive the training they need in a way that best suits their learning style. Furthermore, these platforms often include built-in assessment tools, allowing instructors to track individual progress and identify areas needing additional attention. The data generated by these platforms can be invaluable in assessing the effectiveness of the training program and making necessary adjustments.

Interactive learning platforms also allow for collaboration and peer-to-peer learning, fostering a sense of community and shared responsibility. Recruits can participate in online discussions, share their experiences, and support each other's learning. This sense of community can be particularly valuable during the initial stages of training, when recruits are adapting to a new environment and developing their professional identities. The social learning aspect of these platforms strengthens the cohesiveness of the class and creates a more supportive and collaborative environment.

The use of video technology extends beyond simple lectures and presentations. Consider incorporating high-quality videos of real-world fire incidents – anonymized, of course – into the training program. These videos can provide valuable context, illustrating the realities of firefighting and the importance of the skills being taught. They offer a level of realism that cannot be replicated in a classroom or even a simulation, showing the raw power of fire, the challenges of search and rescue, and the human impact of emergencies. These videos can be incorporated into case studies, encouraging recruits to analyze the incident, identify critical decision points, and discuss potential alternative responses. This approach directly connects the "why" of training to the "how" of real-world application.

Integrating technology into the training program also requires careful consideration of accessibility and equity. It is crucial to ensure that all recruits have access to the necessary technology and support, regardless of their background or circumstances. This may require providing equipment, internet access, or specialized training to ensure everyone can fully participate in the program. Equitable access to technology is not just a matter of fairness; it is essential for creating a diverse and inclusive training environment where all recruits can reach their full potential. This includes providing technical support and appropriate training to all recruits to ensure that they can effectively use the new technologies.

Finally, the effective use of technology requires ongoing assessment and evaluation. It's crucial to regularly evaluate the effectiveness of the technology integrated into the training program and make adjustments as needed. This evaluation should involve feedback from instructors, recruits, and other stakeholders, ensuring the program remains relevant, engaging, and effective. The collection of data on recruit performance, knowledge retention, and overall satisfaction can offer valuable insights into the effectiveness of the technologies utilized.

In conclusion, integrating technology into fire service training isn't about replacing traditional methods, but rather enhancing them to create a more effective and engaging learning environment. By strategically incorporating simulations, interactive learning platforms, and other technological tools, we can strengthen the "why before the how" approach and better prepare recruits for the challenges of this demanding profession. The focus should always remain on the needs of the recruits and the overall goals of the training program, ensuring that the technology enhances and supports the learning process rather than hindering it. Continuous evaluation and adaptation are critical to optimizing the use of technology and maximizing its impact on recruit training.

Creating a supportive and engaging learning environment is paramount to the success of the "why before the how" approach. While the theoretical underpinnings of this methodology are crucial, their effectiveness hinges entirely on how they are received and processed by the recruits. A classroom or training environment characterized by fear, intimidation, or a lack of open communication will actively hinder learning and stifle the very engagement we aim to foster. Conversely, a supportive and encouraging atmosphere where questions are welcomed, mistakes are viewed as learning opportunities, and collaboration is actively promoted will dramatically amplify the effectiveness of the "why before the how" method.

The foundation of a supportive learning environment rests on fostering a culture of trust and mutual respect. This starts with the instructors. Our role extends beyond simply imparting knowledge; we are mentors, guides, and role models. Our demeanor, language, and interactions significantly shape the learning environment. A positive and encouraging tone, even when addressing mistakes, is crucial. Remember, recruits are at various stages of their learning journey. Some may grasp concepts quickly, while others may require more time and patience. Our ability to adapt our teaching style to meet the individual needs of each recruit is essential. This includes recognizing and addressing different learning styles, understanding diverse backgrounds and experiences, and providing individualized support as needed.

Open communication is another cornerstone of a supportive learning environment. We must create a space where recruits feel comfortable asking questions, expressing concerns, and sharing their perspectives without fear of judgment or reprisal. This requires establishing clear communication channels, encouraging open dialogue, and actively soliciting feedback from recruits. Regular check-ins, both individually and as a group, can help to gauge the learning environment's effectiveness and address any emerging concerns promptly. This proactive approach to communication ensures that any potential issues are addressed before they escalate, maintaining a positive and productive learning environment. This also involves being actively receptive to feedback, not just offering it. Regularly solicit feedback from your recruits on what is working, what isn't, and how the training could be improved to better suit their learning styles.

Active participation is key to effective learning, and this requires more than just passive listening. We must design training exercises and activities that actively engage recruits, encouraging them to think critically, problem-solve, and collaborate. This can involve incorporating group projects, simulations, real-world scenarios (where appropriate and safe), and other interactive learning strategies. The use of technology, as discussed previously, provides many excellent avenues for creating engaging and interactive learning experiences. However, technology is simply a tool; its effectiveness depends on how creatively and effectively it is integrated into the training program. The goal is to move away from passive lectures and embrace dynamic and interactive training sessions.

Peer-to-peer learning is a powerful tool that can significantly enhance the learning experience. When recruits learn from and support each other, a sense of community and shared responsibility is developed, strengthening their bonds and fostering a positive learning environment. By working collaboratively, recruits can learn from each other's strengths, share insights, and gain a deeper understanding of the material. This collaborative approach can be integrated into various training activities, including group discussions, team-based exercises, and peer-reviewed assignments. The inherent support structure within the class strengthens the collective learning experience and increases retention. This also helps to build camaraderie and teamwork – skills essential for effective firefighting.

To further cultivate a supportive environment, it is vital to celebrate successes and acknowledge individual progress. This isn't just about rewarding high achievement; it is about recognizing and appreciating the effort and commitment of each recruit. Regular positive reinforcement, both public and private, can significantly impact morale and motivation. This can involve highlighting individual achievements during training sessions, awarding certificates of recognition, or simply expressing sincere appreciation for their hard work and dedication. The recognition doesn't necessarily need to be a grand gesture; small acts of appreciation can go a long way in fostering a positive and supportive learning environment.

Creating a psychologically safe learning environment is equally crucial. Recruits must feel comfortable taking risks, making mistakes, and asking for help without fear of judgment or ridicule. This requires establishing clear expectations regarding behavior, creating a culture of respect and empathy, and providing opportunities for recruits to provide anonymous feedback. Anonymous feedback mechanisms allow recruits to voice concerns or suggestions without fear of reprisal, facilitating a more open and honest dialogue about the training experience. Addressing any concerns promptly and professionally helps to foster a sense of trust and confidence.

Finally, integrating regular feedback loops is fundamental. This involves incorporating various assessment methods, including both formative and summative assessments. Formative assessments provide ongoing feedback throughout the learning process, allowing instructors to identify areas where recruits require additional support. Summative assessments, such as final exams or practical exercises, assess the overall learning outcomes. The feedback received from these assessments should be constructive and tailored to the individual needs of each recruit. This feedback should highlight both strengths and areas for improvement, providing specific and actionable guidance on how to enhance performance. This continuous feedback loop ensures that the training is effective and that the needs of each recruit are addressed throughout the learning process. This also allows for continuous improvement of the training program itself, based on the feedback and performance of the recruits.

In conclusion, implementing the "why before the how" approach requires more than just explaining the rationale behind firefighting techniques. It necessitates the cultivation of a supportive, engaging, and psychologically safe learning environment. By fostering trust, encouraging open communication, promoting active participation, celebrating successes, and integrating regular feedback loops, we can create a training experience that is both effective and inspiring, ultimately preparing the next generation of firefighters for the challenges ahead. Remember, the investment a fire service makes in its recruits extends far beyond financial resources; it's an investment in human potential, and a supportive learning environment is the fertile ground where that potential truly flourishes.

Chapter 3: Assessing and Evaluating Training Effectiveness

Developing effective assessment tools is crucial for determining the success of any training program, and our "why before the how" approach is no exception. The goal isn't simply to test recruits' memorization abilities, but to evaluate their genuine understanding of firefighting principles and their ability to apply that knowledge in practical scenarios. This requires moving beyond traditional, rote-learning assessments and embracing a more holistic and nuanced approach. This approach needs to reflect the modern pedagogical principles that underpin our entire training philosophy.

Traditional methods, often characterized by multiple-choice tests focused solely on factual recall, fall short in assessing the deeper understanding and practical application we aim to foster. A recruit might be able to correctly identify the components of a particular piece of firefighting equipment but lack the understanding of its function within a larger operation. Similarly, they might be able to recite the steps of a particular procedure but fail to execute it effectively under pressure. Such assessments fail to capture the essence of what it means to be a proficient firefighter.

Our assessment strategy must, therefore, be multifaceted, incorporating a variety of tools that comprehensively evaluate recruits' knowledge, skills, and abilities. This includes a careful blend of practical examinations, written tests, and simulations, each designed to address specific learning objectives. Practical examinations should mirror real-world scenarios as closely as possible. This allows us to assess the recruits' ability to apply their theoretical knowledge under conditions that closely resemble the realities of the job. We must move beyond simply observing a recruit perform a task; we must analyze their decision-making process, their problem-solving abilities, and their overall proficiency in executing the procedure safely and effectively.

Consider, for example, a practical examination focused on hose handling and deployment. A simple test might only assess the speed of deployment. However, a more effective assessment would incorporate elements such as teamwork, communication, problem-solving, and safe working practices. Scenarios can be created that introduce unexpected obstacles or challenges, forcing recruits to adapt and improvise, demonstrating their ability to think critically under pressure. This might involve a simulated fire in a confined space, requiring the recruits to coordinate their efforts, manage risks, and make informed decisions based on the situation. The assessment criteria should clearly outline the specific skills being evaluated, ensuring consistency and fairness in the assessment process.

In addition to practical examinations, written tests remain an important component of our assessment strategy, but they must be carefully designed to reflect the "why before the how" approach. Instead of focusing on rote memorization, the questions should probe recruits' understanding of the underlying principles and rationale behind firefighting techniques. Open-ended questions, essay-style responses, and problem-solving scenarios are more effective tools than simple multiple-choice questions in assessing this deeper level of understanding. For instance, instead of asking recruits to list the steps involved in ventilation, we might ask them to explain the principles of ventilation and how different ventilation techniques impact the overall firefighting strategy. This allows us to gauge their comprehension of the underlying concepts and their ability to apply this knowledge to different situations.

Moreover, it's vital to incorporate simulations into our assessment strategy. Simulations offer a controlled environment in which recruits can practice their skills and decision-making abilities without the risks associated with real-world scenarios. This can range from computer-based simulations that replicate fire behavior and building layouts to full-scale simulations involving props and actors that mimic the dynamics of a real fire scene. These simulations provide valuable opportunities for observing recruits' performance under pressure and identifying any areas that require further training or improvement. Careful debriefings following the simulations are critical, providing valuable feedback and a chance to reinforce learning. These debriefings should focus not only on the technical aspects of the performance but also on the recruits' decision-making process, teamwork, and communication skills.

In designing our assessment tools, fairness and relevance are paramount.
Assessments must be aligned with the training objectives and reflect the knowledge, skills, and abilities that are essential for effective firefighting. Bias of any kind must be carefully avoided in the design and implementation of our assessment processes. The assessment criteria should be clearly defined and communicated to recruits well in advance, leaving no room for ambiguity or misinterpretation. Furthermore, the assessments should be designed to accommodate different learning styles and abilities, recognizing that recruits come from diverse backgrounds and have unique strengths and weaknesses. Where

appropriate, accommodations should be made to ensure that the assessments are accessible to all recruits.

The assessment process shouldn't be solely focused on identifying deficiencies; it should also serve as a platform for recognizing and celebrating achievements. Positive reinforcement is essential for boosting morale and encouraging continuous improvement. Providing constructive feedback, tailored to individual needs, is critical to the success of our assessment strategy. This feedback should be specific, actionable, and focused on both strengths and areas for improvement. A well-structured feedback process provides valuable learning opportunities and contributes to the overall development of the recruits. This includes opportunities for self-reflection and peer feedback, encouraging a collaborative approach to learning and development.

Transparency is equally important. Recruits should understand the criteria used to assess their performance and how the feedback relates to their overall progress. This fosters trust and builds confidence in the assessment process. Regularly reviewing the effectiveness of our assessment tools is crucial to ensure that they remain aligned with our training objectives and the needs of our recruits. Regular data analysis should be undertaken, allowing us to identify patterns and trends in performance, adapt our assessments as needed, and continuously improve the quality of our training program. The data gathered through assessments can be used to refine our training methods, addressing specific areas where recruits are struggling and enhancing the overall effectiveness of the program.

Finally, let us remember that the purpose of assessment is not simply to evaluate individual performance but to improve the overall effectiveness of the training program. The data collected from assessments should inform future iterations of the training curriculum, ensuring its continued relevance and adaptability to the ever-evolving demands of the fire service. Our assessment strategies must be seen as an integral part of a continuous improvement loop, where feedback from assessments informs improvements to the training itself, creating a dynamic and responsive training program. By carefully designing and implementing a multifaceted assessment strategy, we can ensure that our recruits are adequately prepared for the challenges they will face as firefighters, while simultaneously enhancing the quality of our training program. The ultimate aim is to empower the next generation of firefighters to approach their profession with both confidence and a deep, principled understanding.

Using data to drive training improvements is paramount in ensuring the efficacy of our "why before the how" approach. The data we collect isn't just a collection of numbers; it's a powerful tool for understanding what works, what doesn't, and how we can continuously refine our training methods to better serve our recruits. This requires a shift from a purely qualitative assessment to a more robust, data-driven approach.

The first step is to identify the key performance indicators (KPIs) that will accurately reflect the success of our training. Traditional metrics, such as pass/fail rates on written exams, offer only a limited perspective. While important, these scores don't necessarily capture the depth of understanding or the practical application of knowledge. Instead, we need to develop KPIs that measure a recruit's ability to apply firefighting principles in real-world or simulated scenarios. This might include metrics such as time taken to complete a task, the efficiency of resource allocation, and the successful execution of complex procedures under pressure. We can also incorporate subjective measures, such as peer and instructor evaluations, which provide valuable qualitative insights into a recruit's overall performance. However, to maximize the value of these subjective evaluations, we need to establish clear, standardized rating scales to ensure consistency and minimize bias. This prevents the subjective aspects of the evaluation from being the primary data source, instead allowing for a complementary view alongside objective performance metrics.

Data collection should be systematic and organized. We can utilize various methods, including electronic record-keeping systems, performance tracking software, and even simple spreadsheets. Whatever method is used, it's critical to ensure that data is collected consistently and accurately. Inconsistent data collection undermines the credibility and usefulness of our analysis. The data should be linked directly to specific learning objectives, allowing us to identify which aspects of the training are most effective and which need improvement. For example, if we notice a significant number of recruits struggle with a particular aspect of ventilation techniques, we can analyze the training materials and instructional methods for that topic, identifying potential areas of weakness.

Once we've collected sufficient data, we can begin the analysis process. This involves examining the data for trends and patterns, comparing performance across different cohorts of recruits, and identifying any correlations between specific training elements and overall performance. Simple statistical analysis can reveal significant insights. For example, we can calculate the average time taken to complete a specific task, identify the range of scores on a practical exam, or analyze the frequency of errors made during simulations. Furthermore, by comparing these metrics across different training groups, we can gain an understanding of the relative effectiveness of various instructional strategies and materials. Analyzing the data will expose which pedagogical methods and learning materials contribute most to improved performance and competency among recruits.

The analysis doesn't stop at identifying areas of weakness; it should also highlight areas of strength. Understanding what aspects of the training are highly effective allows us to replicate and reinforce those successful methods. By meticulously analyzing data from diverse sources, we gain a comprehensive picture of our training program's efficacy. We can use this data to make informed decisions about future curriculum development, resource allocation, and instructional strategies.

However, raw data alone is insufficient. We need to interpret this data within the context of our "why before the how" philosophy. This means examining whether our training methods effectively foster a deeper understanding of the underlying principles of firefighting. This qualitative element is critical to completing the picture of training effectiveness. We need to explore whether our methods facilitate a shift in
the recruits' understanding beyond simply memorizing procedures to comprehending the reasoning behind them.

To achieve this, we can use qualitative methods in conjunction with quantitative data. Post-training surveys, focus groups, and individual interviews with recruits can provide valuable insights into their learning experiences, their understanding of the "why" behind the techniques, and their level of engagement. This will contribute to a more nuanced understanding of our training program's success. Analyzing qualitative feedback can identify areas where our instruction needs improvement in terms of clarity, engagement, and relevance.

For example, we might discover that while recruits are performing well on objective measures, their qualitative feedback reveals a lack of confidence in applying their knowledge in unpredictable situations. This suggests that while the "how" is being mastered, the underlying "why" isn't thoroughly integrated, resulting in a gap between theoretical knowledge and practical application.

This combined quantitative and qualitative data analysis will provide a multifaceted understanding of our training program's effectiveness. This combined analysis will guide the evolution of the training program, ensuring it remains responsive to the needs and learning styles of our recruits. We can adapt our teaching strategies, tailor our materials, and refine our assessment tools to better achieve our training objectives. It's not a static process; continuous improvement should be our guiding principle.

Furthermore, the data analysis should extend beyond the individual recruit level. We need to examine the overall effectiveness of our training program in relation to its impact on departmental performance. This might involve tracking incident response times, the efficiency of resource utilization during emergencies, and the overall safety record of our firefighters. By linking training outcomes to real-world performance, we can demonstrate the direct impact of our program on departmental effectiveness. This demonstrable link between training investment and operational efficiency can justify further investment in the training program and demonstrate its significant return on investment.

Finally, sharing the results of our data analysis with the recruits is crucial. It provides them with valuable insight into their progress, highlighting their strengths and areas for development. This fosters a sense of ownership and accountability, empowering them to take control of their learning. It also promotes a culture of continuous improvement within the department, making everyone part of the training enhancement process. Openly sharing the data establishes transparency and reinforces the program's commitment to continuous improvement.

In conclusion, using data to drive training improvements is not simply about collecting numbers; it's about creating a dynamic, responsive, and ultimately more effective training program. By implementing a systematic data collection and analysis process, we can ensure that our training continually evolves to meet the needs of our recruits and the demands of the fire service. This data-driven approach allows us to move beyond assumptions and anecdotal evidence, establishing a solid foundation for continuous improvement, ultimately enhancing the overall preparedness and performance of our firefighters. The success of our "why before the how" approach depends not only on the innovative pedagogy but also on the rigorous, data-informed evaluation and refinement of our training methodologies.

Tracking student progress effectively requires a multifaceted approach that moves beyond simple pass/fail rates. We need a system that provides both quantitative and qualitative data, offering a comprehensive picture of each recruit's understanding and skill development. This means integrating various assessment methods to capture the breadth and depth of their learning. For instance, regular quizzes focusing on the "why" behind techniques can gauge their conceptual grasp, complementing practical skill assessments that measure their proficiency in executing procedures. These quizzes should be short, frequent, and low-stakes, encouraging continuous learning and reducing the pressure associated with high-stakes summative evaluations. They serve as formative assessments, providing valuable insights into areas where additional instruction or practice may be needed.

Practical skills assessments are equally critical. These could involve simulated scenarios mirroring real-world firefighting situations. These simulations should be meticulously designed to assess specific skills and competencies linked directly to the training objectives. For example, a scenario focusing on building ventilation techniques could evaluate the recruit's ability to identify the optimal ventilation point, safely deploy ventilation equipment, and effectively control the spread of smoke and fire. Observations during these simulations should be recorded using standardized checklists, allowing for objective scoring and easy identification of areas where recruits struggle. It's essential to focus on the process and decision-making behind their actions, not just the outcome, to gain a comprehensive understanding of their understanding. Video recording these scenarios can prove invaluable for both immediate feedback and later analysis, enabling a more detailed review of their performance.

Beyond objective assessments, qualitative feedback is crucial. Regular feedback sessions with individual recruits, perhaps after each practical assessment, offer opportunities for personalized instruction and encouragement. These sessions should focus on a constructive dialogue around their performance, highlighting both their strengths and areas for improvement. The focus should be on understanding the "why" behind their actions – were they applying the underlying principles correctly? Did they understand the rationale behind their chosen approach? These conversations can uncover misconceptions or gaps in understanding that might not be evident from objective assessments alone. Moreover, these sessions foster a strong mentor-mentee relationship, building trust and confidence, and encouraging open communication.

Peer assessment can also be a powerful tool. By having recruits evaluate each other's performance, we encourage active learning and improve their critical thinking skills. This can be incorporated into practical simulations, where recruits analyze each other's techniques and offer constructive criticism, guided by predefined assessment criteria. It's crucial to structure this peer evaluation carefully, emphasizing the importance of respectful and constructive feedback. Training the recruits on providing effective peer feedback is essential to ensure the process is both helpful and fair. The instructor's role in peer assessment is to facilitate and guide the process, ensuring the feedback is objective and focuses on improving the performance.

The data collected from these diverse assessment methods needs to be meticulously organized and analyzed. Spreadsheet software or dedicated learning management systems (LMS) can help track individual progress over time. Graphs and charts can visually represent this data, making it easy to identify trends and patterns. This visual representation is essential for both the instructors and the recruits, enabling them to track progress and identify areas needing improvement. This visual feedback is much more accessible than simply reviewing numerical data and aids the students' ability to understand their improvement.

The use of technology can significantly enhance the tracking and analysis of student progress. LMS platforms allow for automated grading of quizzes, tracking of simulation performance, and the collection of feedback through online surveys. This automated process frees up the instructor's time, allowing for more focused individual attention. Furthermore, technology allows for the creation of customized learning pathways. Based on the progress data, the system can dynamically adjust the training plan for each recruit, focusing on their specific needs and challenges. For example, if a recruit consistently struggles with a particular skill, the system can automatically suggest additional practice exercises or targeted learning modules. This personalized approach helps address the diverse learning styles and paces of each recruit.

Providing timely feedback is paramount to effective learning. Feedback should be both frequent and specific, focusing on concrete behaviors and avoiding vague generalizations. For instance, instead of saying "You need to improve your teamwork," a more effective comment would be, "During the simulated rescue, you didn't effectively communicate your actions to your team members, resulting in a delay in the extraction process. Focus on clearly articulating your plan and seeking confirmation from your team." This constructive approach focuses on specific behaviors and actionable steps for improvement.

Furthermore, feedback should be delivered in a timely manner. Delaying feedback diminishes its impact, allowing time for misconceptions to solidify. Ideally, feedback should be given immediately after an assessment, while the experience is still fresh in the recruit's mind.

Immediate feedback allows for immediate correction and the reinforcement of best practices. This immediate feedback may also prevent the development of incorrect habits or techniques that will be more challenging to correct later in the training. This immediate feedback also allows the recruit to have a better understanding of how to improve on their performance before moving on to the next part of the training.

The feedback process shouldn't be a one-way street. Recruits should actively participate in the feedback discussion, offering their perspective on their performance and asking clarifying questions. This creates a collaborative learning environment, empowering the recruits to take ownership of their learning process. This collaborative approach fosters a culture of open communication and continuous improvement. This mutual feedback fosters a stronger instructor-student relationship, and allows the student to have more ownership over their learning.

Adjusting training methods based on student progress is a crucial component of effective instruction. Regular analysis of the collected data allows instructors to identify areas where the training materials or instructional methods need improvement. If a significant number of recruits struggle with a specific concept or skill, the instructor should review the corresponding training materials and consider revising them to improve clarity and effectiveness. This might involve breaking down complex concepts into smaller, more manageable units, incorporating visual aids or simulations, or changing the teaching approach based on the identified learning challenges. The objective is to make the material more accessible and engaging for all learning styles.

The continuous analysis and adjustment of the training program should be an iterative process. Data from each training cycle should inform the revisions for the following cycle, resulting in a constantly evolving and improving training program. This data-driven approach ensures the program remains relevant and effective, meeting the changing needs of the fire service and the evolving learning styles of recruits. This process of continuous feedback and improvement creates a dynamic training program that consistently adapts and improves. This adaptability ensures that the training program remains relevant and meets the current needs of both the instructors and the students.

In conclusion, tracking student progress and providing personalized feedback are not merely administrative tasks but rather integral components of effective fire service training. By implementing a comprehensive assessment system and leveraging technology to streamline data collection and analysis, we can create a dynamic and responsive learning environment that fosters individual growth and enhances overall departmental performance. This data-driven, personalized approach ensures that we're not just teaching firefighting techniques, but nurturing the next generation of skilled, confident, and passionate fire service professionals. The investment in this data-driven, personalized approach will greatly benefit the individual trainees and the department in the long run, resulting in increased efficiency and overall safety.

Continuous improvement is not merely a desirable trait in fire service training; it's a necessity. The landscape of firefighting, like any other field, is constantly evolving. New techniques emerge, technologies advance, and the challenges faced by firefighters shift. To ensure our training programs remain relevant and effective, we must embrace a culture of continuous evaluation and refinement. This means consistently analyzing the data we collect, soliciting feedback from various sources, and adapting our methods accordingly. It's a cyclical process of assessment, analysis, adaptation, and reassessment, ensuring that our training remains a dynamic and responsive system.

The data collected from the various assessment methods detailed earlier – quizzes, practical simulations, peer evaluations, and instructor observations – provides a rich source of information for program refinement. This data should not be passively stored; it needs to be actively analyzed to identify trends and patterns. For instance, if a significant number of recruits consistently struggle with a particular aspect of ladder deployment, it signals a potential weakness in that section of the training. Similarly, a consistent pattern of poor performance in a specific simulated scenario points to a need for improvement in that area's instruction.

Analyzing this data requires more than just looking at raw scores. We need to delve deeper to understand the *why* behind the numbers. Are recruits struggling because the instructions are unclear? Is the training material too dense or insufficiently illustrated? Are the practice opportunities inadequate? Are the simulations realistic enough to challenge recruits while maintaining a safe environment? These questions are crucial to identify the root causes of performance issues, not just the symptoms.

Technology plays a vital role in this data analysis process. Learning management systems (LMS) can automate the process of data collection and analysis, providing instructors with readily available visualizations of student performance. Graphs and charts can highlight areas of strength and weakness, making it easier to identify trends and focus revision efforts. These visual representations are especially helpful in conveying complex data in a readily understandable format, both for instructors and trainees. They offer a clear picture of the training's overall effectiveness, facilitating evidence-based decision-making in refining the curriculum.

Beyond the quantitative data, qualitative feedback from recruits is indispensable. Post-training surveys, focus groups, and individual feedback sessions offer valuable insights into their learning experience. These qualitative data provide context to the quantitative data, offering explanations for trends and patterns observed. For example, a recruit's feedback might reveal that they understood the theoretical concept but struggled to apply it practically due to a lack of hands-on practice. This type of feedback provides invaluable information for tailoring future training sessions and improving the effectiveness of the program.

Incorporating feedback from instructors is equally important. They are on the front lines of the training process and can offer valuable insights into the strengths and weaknesses of the curriculum. Regular instructor debriefing sessions, where they share their observations and suggestions, can identify areas where materials need clarification, simulations require improvement, or teaching strategies need adjustment. These sessions also provide an opportunity for instructors to share best practices and collaborate on improvements, fostering a culture of continuous learning within the instructor team itself.

The feedback process shouldn't be a one-off event; rather, it should be integrated into the training cycle. Regular check-ins with recruits and instructors should be a routine part of the program, allowing for continuous monitoring and adaptation. This iterative feedback loop ensures the training program remains responsive to the evolving needs and challenges of both the instructors and recruits. This ongoing communication ensures that the training program remains a dynamic and responsive system, reflecting the ever-changing realities of the profession.

Revisions to the training program shouldn't be drastic, wholesale changes. Instead, they should be incremental improvements based on the data and feedback collected. Small adjustments to training materials, minor tweaks to instructional methods, or the addition of supplementary resources can often significantly improve effectiveness. A data-driven approach ensures that these changes are purposeful and impactful, maximizing the return on investment in the training program.

For example, if data shows that recruits consistently struggle with a particular knot-tying technique, the training might incorporate more hands-on practice, the use of instructional videos, or a modified teaching approach. These minor adjustments, guided by evidence, can result in significant improvements in recruit proficiency and confidence. Such refinements demonstrate a commitment to continuous improvement, demonstrating a dedication to enhancing the quality of training and preparing well-equipped firefighters for the demands of the profession.

Another important aspect of program refinement is adapting to the changing needs of the fire service. New technologies, evolving building codes, and updated emergency response protocols necessitate adjustments to the training program. Regular review of industry best practices, participation in professional development opportunities, and interaction with other fire service training organizations can help ensure that the training program remains current and relevant. This ongoing engagement with industry trends ensures the training remains aligned with the ever-evolving needs of the fire service.

Furthermore, continuous improvement involves not just refining existing modules but also exploring new approaches. The incorporation of innovative teaching methods, such as virtual reality simulations or gamified learning modules, can enhance engagement and improve knowledge retention. This constant exploration of new techniques ensures that the program remains at the forefront of training methodologies, providing recruits with the most effective and engaging learning experience.

The process of continuous improvement should be documented. Maintaining a detailed record of revisions made to the training program, including the rationale behind each change, is crucial for accountability and transparency. This documentation serves as a valuable resource for future instructors, ensuring that the program's evolution is well-understood and readily accessible. It also enables a consistent and effective approach to the training, even with changing personnel.

In conclusion, continuous improvement and refinement are not optional extras in fire service training; they are fundamental to its success. By systematically collecting data, seeking feedback from multiple sources, and adapting our methods accordingly, we can create a dynamic and responsive training program that equips firefighters with the skills and knowledge they need to succeed. This commitment to continuous improvement ensures that our training programs remain relevant, effective, and produce the highest quality of fire service professionals.

This commitment reflects a dedication to excellence, prioritizing the safety and well-being of our communities and the success of our firefighters. The ongoing cycle of assessment, analysis, adaptation, and reassessment is not merely a process; it's a commitment to excellence, ensuring that we are constantly striving to improve and evolve. This constant evolution reflects the ever-changing nature of firefighting and the commitment to safety and professionalism.

Benchmarking, in its simplest form, is the process of comparing your organization's performance against that of best-in-class organizations. In the context of fire service training, this means evaluating your department's training programs against those of other departments known for their excellence, effectiveness, and high-performing graduates. This isn't about copying; it's about learning, identifying areas of strength to emulate, and pinpointing weaknesses to address. The goal is to adopt proven strategies and adapt them to your department's unique needs and resources.

The first step in benchmarking is identifying those "best-in-class" organizations. This might involve researching departments renowned for their exceptional training programs, perhaps those with consistently high recruit performance scores on state or national certification exams, or those with a proven track record of producing highly skilled and effective firefighters. Professional organizations like the International Association of Fire Chiefs (IAFC) and the National Fire Protection Association (NFPA) can be invaluable resources in this search. Their publications, conferences, and online forums often highlight exemplary training programs and share best practices.

Once you've identified potential benchmarks, the next step involves gathering data. This could involve reviewing publicly available information on their training programs – their curriculum, training materials, assessment methods, and technology used. Many fire departments are increasingly transparent about their training approaches, making this data readily accessible through their websites or publications.

Participation in professional development workshops or conferences can also provide opportunities to network with personnel from high-performing departments and gain firsthand insights into their training methodologies.

Direct contact with other departments, however, can be the most insightful aspect of benchmarking. This could involve setting up site visits, arranging meetings with training officers, or participating in joint training exercises. Such direct engagement allows for a deeper understanding of their program's nuances, challenges, and successes. It's an opportunity to ask questions, observe training sessions firsthand, and gain a more comprehensive perspective. Remember to approach this interaction respectfully and professionally, clearly stating your intention to learn and improve, not to criticize or compete.

The data collected needs a structured analysis. This involves a comparative review, noting similarities and differences between your department's training program and the benchmark programs. Create a matrix or spreadsheet to organize this information, comparing elements such as:

Curriculum design: Compare the scope and sequence of your curriculum to the benchmarks. Are there crucial topics or skills missing from your program? Are there areas where your curriculum is excessively lengthy or overly complex? Are there innovative teaching approaches used in other departments that could improve your program's effectiveness and engagement?

Training methods: Analyze the teaching methodologies employed in benchmark programs. Do they use a blended learning approach, incorporating both online and in-person instruction? Do they utilize simulations, gamification, or other interactive methods? Are there opportunities to incorporate technology more effectively into your department's training program?

Assessment strategies: How do benchmark departments assess recruit performance? Do they rely solely on written exams, or do they incorporate practical exercises, simulations, and peer evaluations? Are there more effective ways to assess the practical skills and decision-making abilities of your recruits?

Instructor training: How do benchmark departments train their instructors? Do they provide ongoing professional development opportunities for their instructors? Is there room for improvement in the training and development provided to your instructors?

Technology integration: Evaluate the extent to which technology is integrated into benchmark training programs. Do they utilize learning management systems (LMS), virtual reality simulations, or other technological tools to enhance the training experience? Could your department leverage technology to improve the efficiency and effectiveness of its training programs?

Resource allocation: Examine how benchmark departments allocate resources to their training programs. Do they have dedicated training facilities, specialized equipment, and sufficient staffing? Is the level of resource allocation appropriate for the scope and complexity of your department's training needs?

Feedback mechanisms: How do benchmark departments gather feedback from recruits and instructors? Do they use post-training surveys, focus groups, or individual feedback sessions? Are there opportunities to enhance the feedback mechanisms in your department's training programs and make them more robust and effective?

Once the analysis is complete, it's time to develop an action plan. This involves identifying specific areas for improvement within your training program, prioritizing these areas based on their potential impact and feasibility, and developing strategies for implementing the necessary changes. This might involve revising training materials, updating instructional methods, investing in new equipment or technology, or implementing new assessment strategies.

The implementation of these changes must be phased, allowing for ongoing monitoring and evaluation of the effectiveness of the changes being made. This iterative approach allows for ongoing adjustments, adapting the strategies to ensure success. Regular review meetings should be established to track progress, address challenges, and make adjustments as needed.

The results should be meticulously documented, making a clear record of the benchmarking process, the changes implemented, and their impact on recruit performance and overall training effectiveness. This documentation is invaluable not only for internal evaluation but also for future benchmarking efforts and sharing best practices with other departments. This collaborative approach fosters a culture of continuous improvement within the fire service, ensuring that training programs remain dynamic and effective in meeting the evolving demands of the profession. By sharing successes and lessons learned, we create a stronger and safer fire service for all.

Chapter 5: Building a Culture of Continuous Learning

Building a culture of continuous learning within a fire service recruit training program requires more than simply delivering information; it necessitates fostering a growth mindset among recruits. This mindset, characterized by a belief in one's ability to learn and grow, is crucial for navigating the challenges inherent in the profession and for embracing lifelong learning—a cornerstone of success in the dynamic world of firefighting. Transitioning recruits from a fixed mindset, where abilities are seen as innate and unchanging, to a growth mindset requires a strategic and multifaceted approach.

One of the most effective strategies is to explicitly teach the concept of a growth mindset. Recruits should be introduced to the research supporting this idea, understanding that intelligence and abilities are not fixed traits, but rather malleable capacities that can be developed through dedication and effort. This can be achieved through interactive workshops, discussions, and presentations incorporating relevant research and real-world examples from the fire service. For instance, sharing stories of firefighters who overcame challenges through perseverance, highlighting their learning journey, and emphasizing the role of deliberate practice in mastering complex skills can be highly impactful.

Furthermore, the training curriculum itself should reflect the principles of a growth mindset. The emphasis should be on the process of learning rather than solely on the outcome. Instead of focusing exclusively on achieving perfect scores on exams, the curriculum should prioritize the understanding of underlying principles and the development of problem-solving skills. This can involve incorporating activities that encourage experimentation, risk-taking, and learning from mistakes. Simulations, for instance, offer a safe space for recruits to make errors, analyze their actions, and learn from their experiences without real-world consequences. Debriefing sessions following simulations and practical exercises should focus on constructive feedback and identifying areas for improvement, further reinforcing the growth mindset. The focus should be on progress, not perfection.

The use of formative assessment techniques is crucial. Instead of solely relying on summative assessments like final exams, frequent formative assessments, such as quizzes, short assignments, and practical demonstrations, provide continuous feedback to both the instructor and the recruit. This allows for timely intervention and adjustments to the learning process, addressing any gaps in understanding early on. The feedback should be descriptive and specific, highlighting both strengths and areas for improvement, and always framed constructively to encourage effort and perseverance. Furthermore, peer assessment can be an extremely effective tool, allowing recruits to learn from each other and provide support in a collaborative learning environment.

Creating a psychologically safe learning environment is paramount in fostering a growth mindset. Recruits must feel comfortable taking risks, asking questions, and admitting when they don't understand something. This requires instructors to create a culture of trust and respect, where mistakes are viewed as opportunities for learning rather than failures. Active listening, empathy, and patience are essential instructor qualities in this context. Furthermore, encouraging a collaborative learning environment, where recruits work together to solve problems and support each other's learning, is also vital. Group projects, team-based simulations, and peer-to-peer learning opportunities can foster a sense of camaraderie and mutual support.

The language used by instructors plays a crucial role in shaping recruits' mindsets. Instead of focusing on inherent abilities ("You're just not cut out for this"), instructors should emphasize effort and strategies ("Let's explore different approaches to this problem"). Positive reinforcement and encouragement are more effective motivators than criticism or negative feedback. The focus should always be on the recruit's progress and potential for growth, highlighting the journey rather than the immediate destination. Celebrating small victories and acknowledging efforts are essential in fostering a sense of accomplishment and encouraging perseverance.

Incorporating technology can greatly enhance the cultivation of a growth mindset. Online learning platforms, for instance, can provide personalized learning experiences, allowing recruits to learn at their own pace and revisit challenging concepts as needed. Adaptive learning software can tailor the difficulty level to the recruit's individual needs, providing targeted support and preventing frustration. Gamification techniques, such as incorporating points, badges, and leaderboards, can also enhance engagement and motivation. However, it's crucial to use technology thoughtfully, ensuring that it supports, rather than replaces, effective instruction and genuine interaction.

Beyond the classroom, fostering a growth mindset requires a sustained effort from the entire department. Mentorship programs, where experienced firefighters guide and support newer recruits, can provide invaluable guidance and encouragement. Regular feedback sessions between recruits and their supervisors should focus on progress, challenges, and opportunities for growth. Furthermore, promoting a culture of continuous learning within the department as a whole, where professional development is encouraged and supported, will reinforce the growth mindset that's nurtured during initial training. This creates a cohesive environment where lifelong learning is valued and expected, extending the positive impacts of the initial growth-mindset training far beyond the recruit stage.

The successful implementation of these strategies requires a comprehensive approach involving a dedicated team of instructors, supervisors, and departmental leadership. This team should receive training on the principles of a growth mindset and on how to effectively implement these strategies in the training program. Regular evaluation of the program's effectiveness is critical, involving the gathering and analysis of qualitative and quantitative data. This feedback mechanism will provide insights into the effectiveness of the strategies employed and allow for adjustments to optimize the program's impact. The ongoing commitment to fostering a growth mindset is not a one-time initiative but rather an ongoing process that requires sustained effort and a commitment to continuous improvement.

The ultimate aim is not just to train competent firefighters; it's to cultivate a generation of firefighters who are resilient, adaptable, and committed to lifelong learning. By fostering a growth mindset, fire service departments can build a workforce that embraces challenges, thrives in dynamic environments, and is capable of responding effectively to the ever-evolving demands of the profession. This approach translates into a safer and more effective fire service, better equipped to serve and protect the communities they are entrusted to serve. The investment in cultivating this mindset yields significant long-term returns, not only in terms of improved skills and performance but also in terms of increased morale, job satisfaction, and retention rates. In essence, nurturing a growth mindset is an investment in the future of the fire service itself.

Building upon the foundation of a growth mindset established during initial recruit training, we must now consider how to cultivate a culture of continuous learning and professional development that extends far beyond the academy walls. This isn't simply about providing additional training; it's about empowering firefighters to become self-directed learners, actively seeking out opportunities for growth and improvement throughout their careers. This requires a strategic shift in our approach, moving from a model of instructor-led learning to one that fosters autonomy and self-reliance.

One key strategy is to equip firefighters with the tools and resources necessary for self-directed learning. This includes providing access to a comprehensive library of online resources, such as professional journals, online courses, and webinars. Subscription services to relevant publications and access to digital learning platforms can greatly enhance their ability to engage in continuous learning. Furthermore, creating a dedicated space within the fire station, a "learning center" perhaps, equipped with computers, comfortable seating, and a curated collection of relevant materials can make self-directed learning more accessible and appealing. This dedicated space should be promoted as a positive and valuable resource, not simply an afterthought.

Beyond access to resources, we must also foster the skills necessary for effective self-directed learning. This involves teaching recruits how to identify their learning needs, how to locate and evaluate information, and how to apply their knowledge to real-world scenarios. This metacognitive training should be explicitly integrated into the curriculum, providing recruits with strategies for independent learning. For example, workshops on effective research techniques, critical thinking skills, and information literacy can empower them to become more effective self-learners. Regular opportunities for self-reflection and goal setting can help individuals tailor their learning plans to their specific needs and aspirations.

Furthermore, encouraging a culture of peer learning and mentorship within the department is crucial. Experienced firefighters can serve as mentors, guiding and supporting newer members in their professional development. Mentorship programs should be structured and formalized, not relying solely on informal relationships. This ensures that newer recruits have access to valuable guidance and support, especially during challenging times. Peer learning can also take many forms, including study groups, collaborative projects, and informal knowledge sharing. Creating opportunities for firefighters to learn from each other's experiences fosters a strong sense of camaraderie and shared responsibility for continuous learning.

Regular departmental training sessions, however, need to be reimagined. Instead of solely focusing on procedural updates and compliance training, these sessions should also include elements that enhance self-directed learning capabilities. For example, workshops on how to effectively utilize online learning resources or how to create a personal professional development plan can be highly beneficial. Including sessions on time management and prioritization strategies helps firefighters effectively balance their demanding schedules with ongoing professional development activities. These sessions should be interactive and engaging, using a variety of methods to cater to different learning styles.

Incentivizing professional development is also crucial. Offering financial assistance for attending conferences, workshops, or online courses demonstrates a commitment to continuous learning and encourages firefighters to proactively pursue opportunities for growth. Recognizing and rewarding those who actively engage in professional development, perhaps through awards, promotions, or public acknowledgement, further reinforces this culture. This goes beyond simply providing the opportunity; it actively encourages participation and celebrates achievements in professional growth. Incorporating professional development goals into performance reviews further incentivizes firefighters to actively pursue ongoing training and education.

The role of technology in supporting self-directed learning cannot be overstated. Learning management systems (LMS) can provide a central hub for accessing resources, tracking progress, and facilitating communication. These platforms should not only be user-friendly but also mobile-accessible, accommodating the busy schedules of firefighters. The LMS should be integrated into the department's communication systems, making it a readily accessible tool for all members. This ensures easy access to resources, information, and updates on departmental training.

Furthermore, the development of specialized online courses and learning modules tailored to the specific needs of the fire service can enhance self-directed learning. These modules could address topics such as advanced firefighting techniques, hazardous materials response, or leadership and management skills. The use of interactive simulations and virtual reality training can provide a safe and engaging way to practice skills and build confidence. Gamification elements, such as points, badges, and leaderboards, can be used to motivate individuals and foster a sense of friendly competition. But technology should enhance, not replace, the human interaction that is essential to building a strong culture of continuous learning.

Beyond individual development, the department itself should embrace a culture of ongoing learning. Regularly reviewing training materials and procedures ensures relevance and effectiveness. This includes not only updating technical information but also adapting teaching methodologies to better reflect the evolving learning styles of firefighters. Regularly seeking feedback from firefighters on their training needs and preferences ensures that the department's approach remains responsive and relevant. Creating a feedback mechanism that promotes open communication about training effectiveness and individual learning needs is crucial for building trust and mutual understanding.

In conclusion, encouraging self-directed learning and professional development requires a multifaceted approach that integrates technological advancements with a strong commitment to fostering a culture of continuous improvement. This isn't simply about adding more training; it's about empowering firefighters to take ownership of their professional development, fostering a sense of responsibility for their ongoing learning and growth. This creates a more resilient, adaptable, and effective fire service, better equipped to meet the challenges of the 21st century. The investment in this approach yields significant returns not only in improved skills and performance, but also in heightened morale, increased job satisfaction, and improved retention rates. The future of the fire service rests on a foundation of continuous learning, and it is our responsibility to equip the next generation of firefighters with the tools and support they need to thrive in this ever-evolving profession. This sustained commitment to continuous learning, both individually and as an organization, is not merely a worthwhile endeavor; it's essential to the future success and safety of the fire service and the communities it serves.

Building upon the foundation of self-directed learning and readily available resources, we must now delve into the crucial role of mentorship and peer learning in fostering a truly thriving culture of continuous professional development within the fire service. While individual initiative is paramount, the collaborative spirit fostered through mentorship and peer learning significantly amplifies the impact of training and ensures knowledge transfer across generations of firefighters. This isn't merely about pairing experienced personnel with rookies; it's about strategically designing systems that maximize the benefits of shared expertise and create a supportive learning environment.

Effective mentorship transcends the simple transmission of technical skills. A strong mentor-mentee relationship builds trust, fosters open communication, and provides a safe space for the mentee to ask questions, express concerns, and seek guidance, even on matters unrelated to firefighting techniques. The mentor acts as a guide, navigating the mentee through the complexities of the profession, offering both technical and emotional support. This personalized attention can be invaluable, particularly during a recruit's initial years when challenges and uncertainty are most prevalent.

To ensure the success of a mentorship program, careful consideration must be given to the matching process. Mentors should be selected not only for their technical expertise but also for their communication skills, empathy, and ability to build rapport. A mismatch in personalities or learning styles can hinder the effectiveness of the relationship. Similarly, the mentees' individual needs and learning goals should be taken into account when pairing them with a mentor. A structured program with clear goals, timelines, and regular check-ins can help to ensure that the mentorship remains focused and productive. The department should also provide training for mentors on effective mentoring techniques, including active listening, providing constructive feedback, and fostering a supportive learning environment.

Mentorship programs shouldn't be confined to formal, structured relationships. Informal mentoring, where experienced firefighters naturally guide and support newer members, can also play a crucial role in fostering a culture of learning. Creating opportunities for informal interaction, such as shared meals, informal training sessions, and social events, can encourage the organic development of mentoring relationships. These informal interactions can lead to the formation of strong bonds and provide invaluable learning experiences that may not be captured in a formal setting. This informal mentoring can also provide a valuable source of information for recruits on the less formal aspects of department culture, building a stronger sense of belonging.

Peer learning complements mentorship by creating a collaborative learning environment where firefighters of similar experience levels learn from each other. Peer learning can take many forms, from informal knowledge sharing during shift changes to structured study groups focusing on specific topics. Study groups provide a valuable opportunity for firefighters to engage in active recall, test their understanding, and learn from each other's perspectives. The collaborative nature of study groups can make learning more engaging and effective, particularly for those who benefit from interactive learning styles.

The department can actively promote peer learning by creating opportunities for collaboration and knowledge sharing. This could include assigning teams to work on specific projects, organizing workshops or training sessions led by experienced firefighters, or establishing an online forum where firefighters can share information and ask questions. Rotating assignments, allowing firefighters to work with different crews and in different roles, also facilitates peer-to-peer learning by exposing them to diverse perspectives and approaches. Cross-training initiatives, where firefighters receive training in areas outside their immediate expertise, can significantly improve collaboration and interoperability.

Technology can play a crucial role in facilitating both mentorship and peer learning. Learning management systems (LMS) can be used to connect mentors and mentees, track progress, and provide resources. Online forums or collaborative platforms can foster discussions and knowledge sharing among peers. The use of video conferencing technology can enable mentorship relationships to flourish even when mentors and mentees are not in the same location, especially beneficial in larger departments or those spread across multiple stations.

Crucially, the department must actively cultivate a culture that values and supports both mentorship and peer learning. This requires leadership to actively promote these practices, provide the necessary resources, and recognize and reward individuals who participate in these initiatives. Including mentorship and peer learning in performance evaluations can further incentivize participation and underscore their importance within the department. The department needs to recognize that the time spent in mentoring and peer learning is an investment in the future, not a distraction from core duties.

The success of mentorship and peer learning hinges on fostering a culture of openness, trust, and mutual respect. Firefighters need to feel safe expressing their opinions, asking questions, and seeking help without fear of judgment or reprisal. This requires a shift in organizational culture, away from a hierarchical structure towards one that values collaboration and shared responsibility for learning and development. Regular feedback sessions, team-building exercises, and departmental events can all help to cultivate this type of culture. This is also an opportunity to introduce and reinforce the department's values concerning safety, camaraderie, and a commitment to continuous learning.

Regular evaluation of mentorship and peer-learning programs is crucial to ensure their ongoing effectiveness. Gathering feedback from both mentors and mentees can identify areas for improvement and help to refine the programs to better meet the needs of the department. Regularly reviewing and updating the processes, materials, and training associated with these programs is essential to their long-term success. The data collected through these evaluations can inform future program improvements, ensuring that the department continues to invest in developing a high-performing, engaged, and well-trained workforce.

In conclusion, fostering a culture of continuous learning within the fire service requires a multifaceted approach that integrates self-directed learning with the power of mentorship and peer learning. By strategically designing and implementing these programs, departments can create a dynamic and supportive learning environment that benefits both individual firefighters and the organization as a whole. This commitment to collaborative learning is not only an investment in the future of the fire service, but also a testament to its enduring commitment to excellence, safety, and community protection. The lasting impact on individual growth and overall departmental performance justifies the effort and resources dedicated to building and maintaining this robust system of mentorship and peer learning.

Integrating technology into the continuous education of firefighters isn't just about adopting the latest gadgets; it's about strategically leveraging digital tools to enhance learning effectiveness and accessibility. We've established the importance of a robust mentorship and peer learning system, but technology serves as a powerful catalyst, amplifying the reach and impact of these initiatives. It allows us to move beyond the limitations of traditional classroom settings, offering personalized learning experiences tailored to individual needs and learning styles. The modern firefighter, accustomed to instant access to information and interactive online platforms, responds positively to this approach.

One of the most significant advancements in continuing education is the proliferation of online courses. Platforms like Coursera, edX, and numerous fire service-specific providers offer a vast library of courses covering various topics, from advanced firefighting techniques and hazardous materials handling to leadership development and emergency medical services. These courses offer flexibility, allowing firefighters to learn at their own pace and on their own schedule, accommodating the often irregular and demanding nature of shift work.

Furthermore, online courses often incorporate interactive elements, such as quizzes, simulations, and discussion forums, to enhance engagement and knowledge retention. This asynchronous learning allows firefighters to participate in discussions and engage with materials at times convenient to their schedules, addressing the challenges of fitting training into already busy work routines.

The accessibility of online courses is another critical advantage. For smaller departments with limited resources, online courses provide access to expertise and training that might otherwise be unavailable. Geographic location ceases to be a barrier, as firefighters across the country, or even internationally, can access the same high-quality training. This democratization of learning ensures that all firefighters, regardless of their department's size or location, have the opportunity to enhance their skills and knowledge. Departments can curate lists of approved courses, ensuring the quality and relevance of training materials to their specific operational needs. This curated approach also allows departments to track completion and integrate the training into individual performance reviews, further emphasizing the importance of continuous learning.

Webinars represent another powerful tool for integrating technology into continuous education. These live online seminars allow for real-time interaction between instructors and participants, fostering a sense of community and facilitating immediate clarification of doubts. Webinars can cover a wide range of topics, from updates on fire codes and safety regulations to the latest advancements in firefighting techniques. The interactive nature of webinars, often incorporating polls, Q&A; sessions, and chat functions, ensures that participants remain engaged and actively involved in the learning process. This immediacy, the opportunity for real-time questions and answers, addresses a common challenge in traditional training: the inability to immediately address individual learning needs.

To enhance engagement and retention, incorporating interactive simulations into training is crucial. Simulations provide a safe and controlled environment for firefighters to practice their skills and make decisions under pressure, without the risks associated with real-world scenarios. Virtual reality (VR) and augmented reality (AR) technologies are rapidly transforming the way firefighters train, offering immersive and realistic simulations that significantly enhance learning outcomes. These simulations allow trainees to experience complex situations, such as high-rise fires or hazardous material spills, in a risk-free environment, enhancing decision-making skills under duress, something difficult to replicate in traditional training exercises. The ability to repeatedly practice scenarios, adjusting responses and strategies based on immediate feedback, significantly enhances skill acquisition and retention. Data gathered from these simulations can also provide valuable insights into individual and team performance, informing future training needs.

Beyond individual learning platforms, the role of technology in fostering collaborative learning is equally important. Learning management systems (LMS) offer a central hub for storing and managing training materials, tracking progress, and facilitating communication between instructors, mentors, and trainees. These platforms can also incorporate discussion forums, allowing firefighters to share their experiences, insights, and best practices with their peers. This fosters a culture of shared learning, where knowledge is not confined to individual experiences but rather amplified through collaboration and shared knowledge. LMS platforms also allow for easy tracking of individual progress, identifying areas needing further attention or strengthening, improving the effectiveness of the learning process through targeted remediation.

Moreover, the integration of mobile technology offers enhanced accessibility and immediate access to crucial information. Mobile apps can provide firefighters with access to training materials, safety regulations, emergency procedures, and even real-time communication tools. This constant access allows for ongoing reinforcement of learned skills and rapid responses to evolving situations. The integration of mobile technology with departmental communication systems ensures that critical information reaches firefighters promptly, enhancing safety and response effectiveness. Additionally, mobile applications can provide ongoing assessments and quizzes, strengthening retention and allowing for immediate feedback on training and progress.

The effective integration of technology necessitates careful consideration of several factors. First, equitable access to technology is crucial. Departments must ensure that all firefighters have the necessary equipment and internet access to participate in online courses and utilize other digital learning resources. This may involve providing devices, internet subsidies, or creating designated learning spaces within fire stations. Second, adequate training on using the technology is essential. Firefighters must be comfortable and proficient in navigating online platforms, using mobile apps, and participating in virtual simulations. Third, it's crucial to ensure that the chosen technologies integrate seamlessly with existing department systems, preventing information silos and fostering an efficient workflow.

Finally, the selection and integration of technology should be driven by the department's specific training needs and learning objectives. A needs assessment should be conducted to identify the gaps in current training and determine the most appropriate technologies to address these gaps. The selected technologies should align with the department's overall training strategy and should be reviewed and updated regularly to reflect changes in technology and training best practices. Continuous feedback from firefighters is essential in refining the technological integration and ensuring its effectiveness and suitability. The focus should always remain on enhancing the learning experience, not just on the implementation of technology for its own sake. This thoughtful approach ensures that technology truly enhances the effectiveness of continuous learning and contributes to a more skilled, knowledgeable, and adaptable fire service.

Maintaining a vibrant and engaged fire service workforce requires more than just effective initial training; it necessitates a sustained commitment to fostering enthusiasm and passion throughout a firefighter's career. The initial spark ignited during recruit training must be carefully nurtured and fanned into a long-lasting flame. This requires a multifaceted approach that addresses the individual needs and aspirations of each firefighter, while simultaneously cultivating a strong sense of camaraderie and shared purpose within the department.

One crucial element in sustaining enthusiasm is recognizing and rewarding individual achievements and contributions. Simply acknowledging exceptional performance, whether it's mastering a complex technical skill, demonstrating exceptional leadership during an emergency, or consistently going above and beyond in community outreach, can significantly boost morale and motivation. Formal awards ceremonies, departmental newsletters highlighting outstanding achievements, and public recognition during community events all serve as powerful motivators. These acknowledgements underscore the value of individual contributions and foster a sense of pride and accomplishment within the fire service. Moreover, providing opportunities for professional development and advancement reinforces the department's investment in its personnel and cultivates a sense of career progression. Clear career pathways, mentorship programs that connect experienced firefighters with newer recruits, and opportunities for specialized training or leadership roles all contribute to a more engaged and motivated workforce.

Furthermore, fostering a strong sense of camaraderie and teamwork is vital to sustaining enthusiasm. Firefighters often face high-stress situations, and a supportive and collaborative environment can significantly impact their well-being and job satisfaction. Regular team-building activities, both on and off duty, can strengthen bonds and foster a sense of shared purpose. These activities might range from informal social gatherings to more structured exercises focusing on communication, problem-solving, and trust-building within teams. The emphasis should be on creating a culture of mutual respect, support, and open communication, where firefighters feel comfortable sharing their experiences and concerns. This also necessitates a strong emphasis on mental health and well-being within the department. Providing access to mental health resources, fostering open conversations about stress and trauma, and creating a culture of support where seeking help is not stigmatized are crucial for maintaining a healthy and enthusiastic workforce.

Beyond the internal dynamics of the department, actively engaging with the community also plays a significant role in maintaining firefighter enthusiasm. Community outreach initiatives, such as fire safety education programs in schools, public demonstrations of firefighting techniques, and participation in local events, provide firefighters with opportunities to connect with the public and demonstrate the value of their work. This direct interaction with the community fosters a sense of purpose and fulfillment, reinforcing the importance of their role in protecting lives and property. Moreover, these interactions can lead to positive feedback and expressions of gratitude from community members, further boosting morale and motivation.

Continuous learning, as explored in previous chapters, is not merely a means of enhancing technical skills; it's also a powerful tool for maintaining enthusiasm. A firefighter who feels constantly challenged and engaged in learning new skills and techniques is more likely to remain passionate about their profession. Opportunities for advanced training, specialized certifications, and exposure to new technologies all contribute to keeping firefighters stimulated and invested in their career development. Regular training exercises, both on the job and through specialized courses, provide opportunities for skill reinforcement and the acquisition of new knowledge. These activities prevent stagnation and reinforce the importance of continuous professional development.

The development and implementation of innovative training programs are crucial in fostering engagement. Moving beyond traditional lecture-based training methods and incorporating active learning techniques, such as simulations, role-playing, and problem-solving scenarios, can significantly enhance engagement and retention. By shifting the focus from passive absorption of information to active participation and application of learned skills, we can create a more dynamic and motivating learning environment. Moreover, the integration of technology, as discussed previously, can enhance the effectiveness and accessibility of training programs, making continuous learning more convenient and engaging for firefighters.

The role of leadership in maintaining enthusiasm is paramount. Leaders within the fire service have a responsibility to inspire and motivate their personnel, creating a positive and supportive work environment. Effective leaders provide clear direction, offer constructive feedback, and actively seek input from their firefighters. This participatory approach ensures that firefighters feel valued and their concerns are addressed. Leaders should also actively promote a culture of continuous learning and development, providing opportunities for advancement and encouraging firefighters to pursue specialized training and certifications. Open communication, active listening, and a genuine commitment to the well-being of their personnel are essential attributes of effective leaders in the fire service.

Beyond formal leadership roles, peer mentoring and support networks play a significant role in sustaining enthusiasm. Experienced firefighters can act as mentors to newer recruits, sharing their knowledge, experience, and providing guidance. These peer-to-peer relationships can foster a sense of belonging and shared purpose, contributing to a more positive and supportive work environment. Moreover, establishing a culture of shared learning, where firefighters openly share their experiences and best practices, fosters a sense of camaraderie and collective responsibility. This collaborative approach not only strengthens individual skills and knowledge but also enhances team cohesion and efficiency.

Finally, recognizing the sacrifices and dedication of firefighters is crucial to maintaining morale and enthusiasm. The job of a firefighter is demanding and often dangerous, requiring significant personal sacrifices. Acknowledging the challenges and recognizing the commitment of firefighters is paramount. This may involve flexible scheduling where possible, support systems for families, and programs that address work-life balance concerns. Providing access to mental health resources and promoting a culture of open communication about stress and trauma are essential components of supporting the well-being of firefighters and sustaining their passion for the profession. By prioritizing the well-being of firefighters, departments demonstrate their commitment to their personnel and foster a culture of mutual respect and appreciation. This, in turn, significantly enhances job satisfaction and sustains the long-term enthusiasm and passion for the challenging and rewarding profession of firefighting.

Chapter 6: Addressing Common Challenges in Recruit Training

Implementing any significant change within an established system, particularly one as ingrained as traditional fire service training, inevitably encounters resistance. This resistance isn't necessarily born from malice or a lack of dedication; it often stems from deeply held beliefs, ingrained habits, and a justifiable concern about maintaining established standards of excellence. Experienced instructors, having honed their craft over years of experience, may view new methodologies with skepticism, particularly when they deviate from practices that have demonstrably yielded success in the past. Understanding these underlying causes is the first step in navigating this resistance and fostering a smooth transition to more effective training techniques.

One common source of resistance is the perceived threat to established expertise. Instructors who have spent years mastering their delivery style and curriculum may feel their skills are being undervalued or dismissed by the introduction of new approaches. This feeling is exacerbated by the inherent emotional investment instructors have in their teaching methods. Their approach represents not only a professional skillset, but a personal expression of their dedication to the profession. Challenging this deeply ingrained methodology can be interpreted as a personal affront, hindering the acceptance of new strategies. To address this, it's crucial to frame the new approach not as a replacement but as a complement. The emphasis should be on enhancing, not replacing, existing expertise. Workshops and training sessions designed to introduce instructors to modern pedagogical approaches should highlight how these techniques can build upon their existing skills, allowing them to refine and expand their capabilities rather than discard them entirely. Open and honest communication is critical. Instructors should be actively involved in the process of adopting new methods, providing input and feedback at every stage. This collaborative approach not only ensures buy-in, but also leverages their invaluable experience to refine and tailor the new training approach to the specific needs of the department.

Another significant hurdle is the lack of time and resources often available for professional development. Instructors are already burdened with heavy workloads and responsibilities. The prospect of additional training to master new teaching methods can feel overwhelming, especially when there's no immediate visible benefit. This lack of time can foster resentment towards initiatives perceived as adding to an already significant workload. To address this, professional development should be approached strategically, prioritizing a gradual implementation of new techniques rather than a complete overhaul. Short, focused workshops or online modules can be integrated into existing schedules without significantly disrupting day-to-day operations. Moreover, access to readily available online resources and peer-to-peer support networks can significantly reduce the burden of learning new skills. By strategically scheduling professional development opportunities and providing ample support resources, the perceived burden of change can be substantially reduced, encouraging a more receptive attitude towards new training approaches.

Furthermore, instructors may be resistant to change simply due to a lack of understanding or familiarity with the new methodologies. Many traditional instructors may be unfamiliar with modern pedagogical theories and their application in practical training scenarios. This lack of familiarity can breed uncertainty and apprehension, fueling resistance to the adoption of new techniques. Providing comprehensive training, encompassing both theoretical foundations and practical application, is crucial to alleviate this concern. This training should utilize a variety of methods, including demonstrations, interactive exercises, and peer-to-peer learning opportunities, to ensure a thorough grasp of the new approaches. Furthermore, access to ongoing support and mentorship from experienced trainers who have successfully implemented these techniques can provide instructors with the confidence and guidance they need to confidently integrate the new methods into their teaching. The key here is to provide a structured learning experience that bridges the gap between theory and practice, fostering a deep understanding and the confidence to successfully adopt new techniques.

A common concern amongst instructors is the potential disruption to established routines and comfort zones. Years of experience have often created deeply ingrained habits and routines. The introduction of new methodologies can disrupt these established patterns, creating uncertainty and anxiety. This resistance stems not from a lack of willingness to improve, but from a natural aversion to change and a preference for the familiar. To mitigate this, change management should be approached strategically, emphasizing a gradual transition rather than an abrupt shift. Phased implementation, starting with small-scale pilot programs, allows instructors to adapt to the new methods incrementally, minimizing disruption and anxiety. Moreover, fostering a culture of open communication and feedback is critical. Regular meetings and open forums allow instructors to voice their concerns, share their experiences, and contribute to the refinement of the new training approach. This collaborative approach not only reduces resistance but also leverages the valuable insights of experienced instructors, leading to a more effective and tailored training program.

Another potential obstacle is the perceived lack of relevance or practicality of the new methods. Instructors may question the effectiveness of new approaches, particularly if they don't see a direct correlation to improved firefighter performance. This skepticism can be particularly pronounced when new methods require significant shifts in teaching style or the use of unfamiliar technology. Addressing this concern necessitates clear and demonstrable evidence of the new methods' effectiveness. Data on improved student engagement, increased test scores, and enhanced practical skills should be collected and shared to demonstrate the tangible benefits of the new approach. Furthermore, successful case studies and examples from other fire departments that have implemented similar programs can provide compelling evidence of the effectiveness of these modern pedagogical techniques. By providing concrete evidence of the positive outcomes, the perceived lack of relevance and practicality can be effectively addressed, paving the way for a more receptive attitude toward change.

Moreover, the organizational culture itself can significantly influence the level of resistance to change. In some fire departments, a hierarchical structure and a strong emphasis on tradition can create an environment that is less receptive to new ideas. This resistance isn't necessarily intentional but arises from a deep-seated cultural preference for established methods and a reluctance to deviate from well-trodden paths. To counter this, leadership must actively champion the adoption of new methods. This involves clear communication of the rationale behind the change, active engagement with instructors during the implementation process, and a visible commitment to supporting their professional development. Creating a culture of continuous improvement and innovation, where new ideas are encouraged and feedback is valued, is crucial for fostering a positive environment for change. Furthermore, recognizing and rewarding instructors who embrace new methods can help establish the adoption of these techniques as a valued and respected practice within the department.

Finally, it is imperative to address the potential for misinformation and skepticism among instructors. This can often stem from misinterpretations of the intended changes, fear-mongering by those resistant to change, or a lack of clear communication from leadership. To counter this, a proactive communication strategy is crucial. This involves providing instructors with clear, concise, and accurate information about the new methods, addressing their concerns openly and honestly, and providing opportunities for open discussion and feedback. Transparency in the decision-making process and a demonstrable commitment to addressing instructor concerns are vital for building trust and overcoming any misinformation or skepticism that may arise. By proactively addressing these potential challenges, the department can significantly improve the likelihood of a successful transition to a more modern and engaging training approach, resulting in improved recruitment, training, and ultimately, firefighter performance. The success of this transition hinges not just on the effectiveness of the new methods themselves, but on the careful and thoughtful management of the inevitable resistance to change.

The success of any training program hinges on its ability to effectively reach every individual. In the fire service, where lives depend on the competence and readiness of personnel, this is paramount. Recognizing that recruits arrive with diverse backgrounds, learning preferences, and prior experiences is crucial to crafting an inclusive and impactful training curriculum. A one-size-fits-all approach, often associated with traditional lecture-heavy methods, risks alienating some learners and hindering the overall effectiveness of the program. This is particularly true in today's environment, where recruits are accustomed to interactive digital learning experiences and expect a more engaging and dynamic educational journey.

The modern recruit is frequently more comfortable navigating online platforms and digital learning tools than with traditional methods. Many have experienced self-directed learning environments, fostering a sense of autonomy and control over their educational journey. To engage this demographic effectively, incorporating digital learning platforms, interactive simulations, and online learning modules can significantly enhance engagement and provide learners with opportunities to learn at their own pace. Online quizzes, interactive videos explaining complex concepts through realistic scenarios, and virtual reality (VR) training exercises can enhance the learning experience, appealing to those who thrive in technology-driven learning spaces. This isn't simply about incorporating technology for the sake of it; it's about leveraging technology to create a more accessible, engaging, and personalized learning environment.

Beyond digital fluency, recruits may possess diverse learning styles. Some are visual learners, benefiting from diagrams, charts, and demonstrations. Others are auditory learners, grasping information best through lectures, discussions, and audio recordings. Still others are kinesthetic learners, preferring hands-on activities, simulations, and practical application to absorb new knowledge. A comprehensive training program must cater to these varied preferences. Consider incorporating a wide array of teaching methods – lectures supplemented by visual aids, hands-on exercises with detailed explanations, group discussions, and individual practice sessions. This multimodal approach ensures that every learner, regardless of their preferred learning style, has opportunities to engage with the material in a way that resonates with them.

Furthermore, individual learning needs can vary significantly due to factors like prior experience, educational background, and even personal learning disabilities. Some recruits may possess prior experience in related fields, while others may lack foundational knowledge. Some might have exceptional spatial reasoning skills, while others may require more explicit instructions and repetition. A robust training program will acknowledge and address these differences. Pre-training assessments can identify individual strengths and weaknesses, allowing instructors to tailor their approach and provide targeted support where needed. This could involve individualized learning plans, supplemental resources, or additional one-on-one instruction. This personalized approach not only ensures that every recruit receives the support they need, but it also fosters a sense of inclusivity and respect for individual learning journeys.

Adaptive learning technologies can also play a vital role in addressing diverse learning needs. These platforms adjust the difficulty and pace of instruction based on the individual learner's performance, providing customized learning paths. They can identify knowledge gaps and provide targeted remediation, ensuring that every recruit masters the essential skills and knowledge. This is particularly useful when teaching complex procedures or technical concepts that require a thorough understanding before moving to practical application. The use of such tools, integrated within a broader multimodal approach, can dramatically improve learning outcomes for all recruits, regardless of their background or learning styles.

It's essential to create a supportive and inclusive learning environment where recruits feel comfortable asking questions, seeking clarification, and admitting when they need additional support. The training environment should be one that promotes open communication and collaboration. Group activities, peer-to-peer learning opportunities, and constructive feedback sessions can all contribute to a more inclusive and supportive classroom. Encouraging recruits to actively participate in their learning process empowers them, fosters a sense of ownership over their education, and ultimately improves learning outcomes. This sense of community and shared learning journey can also enhance team cohesion and build camaraderie among recruits, fostering a collaborative spirit that translates to improved teamwork on the job.

However, addressing diverse learning styles and needs goes beyond simply offering a range of teaching methods. It requires a shift in instructor mindset and a commitment to ongoing professional development. Instructors must be equipped with the pedagogical knowledge and skills to effectively adapt their teaching strategies to meet the needs of individual learners. This means moving beyond the traditional lecture format and embracing a more learner-centered approach. The focus should be on fostering understanding, encouraging critical thinking, and providing opportunities for active participation. This may involve incorporating active learning techniques such as case studies, problem-solving scenarios, and simulations that challenge recruits to apply their knowledge in realistic situations. These approaches can significantly enhance knowledge retention and practical skills development.

Furthermore, instructors should receive ongoing professional development opportunities focused on modern pedagogical approaches and strategies for adapting instruction to meet diverse learning needs. This training should encompass a range of topics including differentiated instruction, universal design for learning (UDL), and assessment strategies that accurately measure student learning. Providing ongoing professional development ensures that instructors are continually refining their skills and adapting their methods to enhance the learning experience for all recruits. This ensures not only better training but also a demonstration of commitment to professional excellence within the department.

Regular feedback mechanisms are also essential for gauging the effectiveness of the training program and identifying areas for improvement. This could involve student feedback surveys, instructor observations, and performance assessments. The data collected through these mechanisms can be used to inform instructional decisions, ensuring that the program remains responsive to the changing needs of recruits and the evolving demands of the fire service profession.

Beyond the formal learning environment, the department should also encourage a culture of continuous learning and professional development. Providing access to online resources, professional development opportunities, and mentoring programs allows recruits to continue learning and developing their skills long after they complete their initial training. This approach not only improves individual competency but also ensures that the department as a whole remains at the forefront of the ever-evolving fire service landscape.

In conclusion, effectively managing diverse learning styles and needs in recruit training requires a comprehensive and multifaceted approach. It requires not only the incorporation of modern pedagogical methods and technologies but also a fundamental shift in the way instructors approach training. By embracing a learner-centered approach, fostering an inclusive learning environment, and providing ongoing professional development for instructors, fire departments can significantly enhance the effectiveness of their recruit training programs, equipping future firefighters with the skills and knowledge necessary to excel in their demanding profession. The investment in diverse learning methodologies ultimately translates into a more proficient, resilient, and capable fire service, better prepared to respond to the complex challenges of the modern world. This commitment to robust, adaptive training is not just an investment in individual firefighters; it's an investment in the safety and well-being of the entire community.

Addressing the realities of limited time and resources within a fire service training department requires a strategic and innovative approach. The ideal scenario, with limitless time and abundant resources, allows for extensive exploration of various teaching methods and the implementation of cutting-edge technology. However, most fire departments operate within budgetary constraints and often face scheduling pressures. The good news is that impactful training doesn't necessitate a massive financial outlay or an unrealistic restructuring of the training calendar. The key lies in prioritizing and optimizing existing resources while strategically integrating cost-effective and time-efficient solutions.

One crucial element is to meticulously analyze the existing curriculum. This necessitates a frank assessment of what truly needs to be taught, and perhaps more importantly, what can be streamlined or even eliminated. Many training programs have accumulated content over time, resulting in a bloated curriculum that overwhelms recruits and stretches training schedules thin. By critically evaluating each component of the curriculum, identifying redundancies, and focusing on core competencies, departments can create a more focused and impactful program without sacrificing essential skills. This involves prioritizing what's most critical for immediate job performance, focusing on essential skills and knowledge, rather than trying to cover everything at once.

This targeted approach allows for a greater depth of coverage in the areas that truly matter, leading to better knowledge retention and practical application. For instance, instead of superficially covering every conceivable type of rescue scenario, the training could focus on core rescue techniques that are most frequently encountered.

This allows for more realistic simulations and hands-on practice, enhancing the recruits' skills and confidence in handling these situations effectively.

A systematic approach to curriculum review can involve creating a matrix that lists each training module, its objectives, the time allocated, and an evaluation of its relevance and impact. This data can then be used to identify areas for streamlining or consolidation. Departments can use data analysis of past recruit performance to help in this assessment. Which training modules lead to the best outcomes? Which result in lower scores or poorer performance in practical applications? This data provides the evidence-based framework for trimming unnecessary content and enhancing effectiveness. Furthermore, input from experienced firefighters and instructors, coupled with feedback from past recruits, can offer valuable insights and perspectives on the effectiveness of the current training.

Once the core curriculum has been defined, instructors can then explore efficient methods of delivery. Instead of solely relying on lengthy lectures, consider incorporating short, focused presentations combined with interactive activities, simulations, and hands-on practice. This active learning approach enhances engagement and retention, making the training more effective even with reduced time. This approach respects the recruits' time and keeps them engaged and motivated, making the overall training process more efficient and successful.

Technology can be a powerful ally in addressing time and resource constraints. While expensive high-fidelity simulators may be out of reach for some departments, there are many readily available, cost-effective digital tools that can significantly enhance training. Online learning platforms, for example, can deliver essential background information, allowing for classroom time to be dedicated to hands-on practice and practical application. Interactive online quizzes and simulations can assess understanding and reinforce learning in a time-efficient manner. Short, targeted videos demonstrating critical techniques can replace lengthy, potentially less engaging, lectures. These digital resources can be accessed by recruits at their own pace, fitting seamlessly into their schedules, enhancing flexibility.

Moreover, the use of readily accessible digital resources can minimize the dependence on costly printed materials. The environmental impact is significantly reduced, and the constant accessibility makes updating and revising materials significantly simpler. This flexibility is crucial in the rapidly evolving field of fire service, where techniques and procedures are regularly updated to reflect best practices and technological advancements.

Furthermore, fostering a culture of peer-to-peer learning can significantly reduce the instructor's workload and enhance the learning experience. By incorporating group activities, peer instruction, and mentorship opportunities, recruits can learn from each other's experiences and perspectives. This approach not only reduces the instructor's time commitment but also enhances team cohesion and strengthens bonds between recruits, ultimately improving teamwork. Creating an environment where collaborative learning flourishes is crucial to effective and efficient training. Recruits can teach each other, enhancing their learning, and the overall cost of training is dramatically lowered.

105.

Addressing time and resource limitations also requires a commitment to ongoing professional development for instructors. Providing instructors with access to training on effective teaching methodologies, including those specifically tailored to adult learners and those reflecting the latest advancements in fire service practices, enhances their abilities to deliver engaging and efficient training. Regular training workshops focused on maximizing impact with limited time and resources, can equip instructors with the tools and strategies needed to optimize their teaching practices. This investment in instructor training pays dividends in the long run, leading to more efficient and impactful training for recruits.

Finally, effective communication and collaboration between training officers and other department personnel are paramount. Open communication channels and regular meetings can facilitate the identification of potential scheduling conflicts and resource allocation challenges. Collaboration with other departments might offer opportunities for sharing resources or collaborating on training exercises, thereby maximizing efficiency and minimizing costs. This proactive approach ensures that the training program is integrated into the broader operational framework of the department, avoiding conflicts and enhancing efficiency.

In summary, addressing time and resource constraints in fire service recruit training requires a combination of strategic planning, creative problem-solving, and a commitment to continuous improvement. By meticulously analyzing the curriculum, incorporating cost-effective technologies, fostering a culture of peer-to-peer learning, and investing in instructor training, fire service departments can overcome these challenges and deliver high-quality, impactful training that prepares recruits for the demands of their challenging and vital profession. This strategic approach ensures that the limitations of resources do not compromise the quality and effectiveness of the training provided. The focus should always remain on providing recruits with the knowledge, skills, and confidence to excel in their roles as dedicated and competent firefighters. Investing in efficient and effective training is, ultimately, an investment in community safety.

Dealing with unmotivated or difficult recruits requires a nuanced approach that goes beyond simple disciplinary measures. It demands a deep understanding of adult learning principles and a willingness to adapt teaching strategies to meet individual needs. The first step involves identifying the root cause of the disengagement. Is it a lack of interest in the profession, personal challenges impacting their ability to focus, learning differences that haven't been addressed, or perhaps a disconnect with the training methods employed?

Effective communication is crucial. Instead of resorting to criticism, initiate open and honest conversations with the recruit. Create a safe space where they feel comfortable expressing their concerns and frustrations without fear of reprisal. Active listening is paramount; understand their perspective before attempting to offer solutions. This requires patience and empathy. The goal is not to judge but to understand the underlying issues hindering their progress.

Once the root cause is identified, a tailored intervention can be developed. For example, a recruit struggling with the technical aspects of firefighting might benefit from one-on-one tutoring or access to supplementary learning materials. Those lacking intrinsic motivation might respond well to a clear demonstration of the real-world application of the skills they're learning. Taking them on ride-alongs, shadowing experienced firefighters, or showing videos of actual emergency responses can help them connect the training to the reality of the job. This can transform abstract concepts into tangible experiences, sparking enthusiasm and fostering a deeper understanding of the importance of their training.

Addressing learning differences is another critical aspect. Some recruits may benefit from visual aids, others from hands-on activities, and still others from auditory learning techniques. A diverse range of learning strategies is essential to cater to different learning styles. This necessitates a flexible and adaptable teaching methodology, moving beyond the traditional lecture format and incorporating interactive exercises, group work, and simulations. The use of technology, such as interactive learning platforms and virtual reality simulations, can also play a significant role in engaging recruits with diverse learning needs. The key is to ensure that every recruit has the opportunity to learn and succeed in a manner that resonates with their individual strengths and preferences.

For recruits struggling with personal challenges impacting their ability to focus, a compassionate and supportive approach is essential. It's important to maintain a professional yet understanding demeanor, recognizing that personal issues can significantly affect a person's ability to concentrate and learn. Referring them to appropriate support services within the department or community can be beneficial. This might include counseling, mentoring programs, or access to resources that address specific needs. This demonstration of care and concern can foster a sense of trust and encourage them to seek help. Addressing personal challenges doesn't diminish the standards expected, but it provides a framework of support to help the recruit overcome obstacles and succeed.

Creating a positive and supportive learning environment is crucial. Positive reinforcement, acknowledging effort and progress, is far more effective than constant criticism. Celebrating successes, both large and small, helps build confidence and encourages continued engagement. This fosters a culture of mutual respect and trust, promoting a more conducive atmosphere for learning. Providing regular feedback, delivered constructively and focused on specific areas for improvement, empowers the recruits to track their progress and work toward their goals. The focus should always be on progress, not perfection. This approach builds self-efficacy and strengthens their commitment to the training.

Sometimes, despite best efforts, some recruits may remain disengaged. In such cases, a frank discussion about their commitment to the profession is necessary. This discussion should be handled with sensitivity, ensuring the recruit feels heard and respected. If the disengagement stems from a lack of interest or an incompatibility with the profession, it's crucial to address this openly. While it may be difficult, recognizing that some recruits may not be the right fit for firefighting can save both the individual and the department resources. A structured process for addressing this, with clear pathways for potential alternative roles or exiting the program, should be established. This provides a respectful and supportive framework, ensuring fair treatment for all individuals involved.

For those recruits who demonstrate consistently disruptive behavior, a clear and consistent disciplinary process needs to be in place. This process should be fair and transparent, with clear expectations and consequences communicated upfront. While disciplinary measures are sometimes necessary, they should be employed as a last resort, after other strategies have been attempted. Maintaining open communication, actively listening to concerns, and providing support whenever possible are essential aspects of fostering a respectful and productive training environment. In the event of disciplinary action, the focus should always be on correcting behavior and supporting the recruit's overall development, not on punishment. The goal is to foster a climate of accountability, ensuring professional standards are maintained without compromising the well-being of the recruits.

Regular evaluation of the training program is crucial. Gathering feedback from both recruits and instructors provides valuable insights into areas that require improvement. This feedback can be used to refine teaching methods, adapt the curriculum to meet the needs of the recruits, and enhance the overall effectiveness of the program. This iterative process of continuous improvement ensures that the training remains relevant, engaging, and impactful. By consistently adapting to the needs of the recruits, the training program can maximize its impact and ensure that all recruits have the opportunity to develop the skills and knowledge necessary to excel as firefighters.

In conclusion, addressing challenges posed by unmotivated or difficult recruits requires a multi-faceted approach that prioritizes understanding, communication, and support. By implementing a combination of effective teaching strategies, tailored interventions, and a supportive learning environment, fire service training departments can enhance engagement and improve outcomes. This inclusive approach not only benefits the individual recruits but also strengthens the overall fire service, ensuring that the next generation of firefighters are well-prepared to serve their communities effectively and efficiently. Remember, investing in the development of recruits is an investment in public safety. A strong, well-trained team is the foundation of a robust and reliable emergency response system.

Maintaining a safe training environment is paramount during hands-on exercises. The inherent risks associated with firefighting necessitate a rigorous approach to safety protocols, encompassing pre-training preparation, meticulous execution, and thorough post-training debriefing. Negligence in this area can lead to injuries, equipment damage, and a breakdown in trust and confidence. Our commitment to safety must be unwavering; it's not merely a checklist item but a fundamental principle underpinning all our training activities.

Before any hands-on activity commences, a comprehensive risk assessment is essential. This involves identifying all potential hazards associated with the specific exercise. For instance, during live fire training, potential hazards include burns, smoke inhalation, falls from heights (if ladder drills are involved), equipment malfunctions, and injuries from tools or falling debris. With confined space training, the risks include oxygen deficiency, hazardous atmospheres, entrapment, and structural collapse. For vehicle extrication scenarios, the dangers include crushing injuries from hydraulic tools, entanglement in vehicle parts, and electrocution. A detailed analysis of each scenario is required to identify all potential risks.

Once the hazards are identified, we must develop and implement control measures. This might involve providing the appropriate personal protective equipment (PPE), such as turnout gear, SCBA, gloves, and eye protection. Detailed safety briefings before each exercise are mandatory, clearly outlining the potential risks, the appropriate safety procedures, and emergency protocols. Designated safety officers should be present at all times to oversee the exercises, ensuring adherence to safety regulations and intervening immediately in case of any incidents. These safety officers should be experienced personnel who are not only well-versed in firefighting techniques but also possess a deep understanding of safety procedures and emergency response. Their role extends beyond passive observation; they must actively monitor the participants' actions, providing guidance and corrections as needed.

The training area itself requires careful consideration. The location should be chosen to minimize the risks associated with the specific training exercise. Sufficient space must be available to accommodate all participants and equipment safely. Obstacles and potential trip hazards should be removed or clearly marked. Adequate lighting and communication systems are also crucial. For live fire training, a designated safety zone must be established well outside the training area, providing a safe haven for participants and observers. Regular inspections of the training area are necessary to ensure its continued safety. This includes checking for any structural weaknesses, potential fire hazards, and ensuring the proper functioning of safety equipment.

The use of appropriate equipment is another key factor in maintaining safety. All equipment must be regularly inspected and maintained according to manufacturer guidelines. Faulty or malfunctioning equipment should be removed from service immediately. Participants must receive comprehensive training on the proper use and care of all equipment before engaging in any hands-on activities. This training should include demonstrations, practical exercises, and written tests to ensure they understand and can correctly use all equipment involved. Moreover, participants should be familiar with the emergency shutdown procedures for all equipment, such as hydraulic tools or generators.

Effective communication is vital during any hands-on training. Clear communication channels must be established to ensure swift and efficient responses in case of any emergencies. Participants should be instructed to use clear and concise radio communication to alert safety personnel of any issues. Designated emergency response procedures should be in place for each type of training, clearly defining roles and responsibilities for all participants and safety personnel. Regular drills should be conducted to reinforce these procedures and ensure their effectiveness. This fosters a culture of preparedness and helps instill confidence among participants in their ability to handle emergencies effectively.

After each hands-on exercise, a thorough debriefing is essential. This involves a critical review of the exercise, focusing not only on the technical skills but also on safety practices. Participants should be encouraged to openly discuss any safety concerns or near misses that occurred during the exercise. This open communication is invaluable in identifying areas where safety procedures can be improved. The debriefing is an opportunity to learn from any mistakes made and to reinforce good safety practices. It also serves as a platform to identify and address any specific safety concerns related to individual participants' performance.

Further enhancing safety involves employing modern training aids and techniques. Virtual reality simulations, for instance, can provide realistic training scenarios without the inherent risks of live fire or other high-hazard environments. These simulations allow participants to practice critical skills in a controlled and safe environment, repeating scenarios multiple times without fear of injury or equipment damage. Similarly, interactive computer-based training programs can enhance theoretical knowledge and build a foundational understanding of safety procedures before engaging in hands-on exercises.

Moreover, incorporating regular medical checkups and fitness evaluations for all participants is crucial. This ensures that recruits are physically and medically fit for the demands of firefighting training. Identifying any underlying health conditions early on prevents potential hazards during high-intensity exercises. This proactive approach demonstrates a department-wide commitment to the well-being of all personnel. Pre-existing conditions should be carefully considered during the risk assessment process, adapting training exercises as needed to accommodate individual needs while maintaining a safe training environment.

Furthermore, a continuous improvement cycle is necessary for maintaining optimal safety. Regularly reviewing incident reports, gathering feedback from participants and safety officers, and conducting post-incident analyses are essential for identifying areas requiring improvement. This data-driven approach to safety allows for continuous adjustments to training protocols, ensuring that safety measures remain effective and up-to-date. The feedback gathered should be used to modify training plans, update safety procedures, and improve the overall safety culture within the department. This commitment to continuous improvement signifies that safety is not a static condition but a dynamic process that requires ongoing attention and adaptation.

Finally, a robust reporting system for safety incidents, near misses, and hazards is essential. A clear and accessible system should be in place for reporting any safety concerns or incidents, ensuring prompt investigation and remedial action. This system needs to be transparent and non-punitive, encouraging reporting without fear of reprisal. Analysis of this data allows for the identification of trends and recurring safety issues, enabling the department to proactively address potential problems before they result in serious incidents. This proactive approach is vital for fostering a safety-conscious culture within the fire service and ensuring the well-being of all personnel. Ultimately, prioritizing safety is not just a legal requirement but an ethical imperative, reflecting our commitment to the well-being of our recruits and the success of our training program. Every precaution taken, every protocol followed, every safety measure implemented reinforces our dedication to ensuring a safe and effective learning environment for all.

Chapter 7: The Instructor's Role in Shaping Future Firefighters

Inspiring a passion for the fire service goes beyond simply imparting technical skills; it's about igniting a fire within each recruit, fostering a deep sense of purpose and commitment to the profession. This requires instructors to move beyond the traditional lecture format and embrace a more holistic approach to teaching. It's about connecting with recruits on a personal level, understanding their motivations, and helping them discover the profound impact they can have on their communities. This involves creating a learning environment that is not just safe and effective but also engaging, challenging, and inspiring.

One of the most effective ways to inspire passion is through storytelling. Sharing real-life accounts of heroism, resilience, and the profound impact firefighters have on people's lives can powerfully resonate with recruits. These stories humanize the profession, moving beyond the technical aspects and highlighting the emotional rewards of serving others in times of crisis. We can showcase examples of firefighters going above and beyond the call of duty, displaying courage, compassion, and unwavering dedication. These narratives serve as powerful reminders of the profound difference firefighters make in the lives of individuals and communities.

Furthermore, fostering a strong sense of camaraderie and teamwork among recruits is crucial. Firefighting is inherently a team-based profession, and fostering strong interpersonal relationships enhances performance and morale. Instructors can implement team-building exercises, group projects, and collaborative problem-solving activities to strengthen bonds among recruits. This approach goes beyond academic learning; it cultivates a sense of belonging, mutual respect, and shared purpose within the group. The collaborative spirit built during training translates directly to operational effectiveness, enhancing the team's ability to work together seamlessly during emergencies.

Mentorship plays a significant role in cultivating a passion for the profession. Pairing experienced firefighters with new recruits provides invaluable guidance and support, helping them navigate the challenges and rewards of firefighting. Mentors can serve as role models, sharing their experiences, offering advice, and providing encouragement. This personalized approach addresses the individual needs of each recruit, building confidence and a sense of belonging. Moreover, the mentoring relationship fosters continuous learning, encouraging recruits to seek out new knowledge and skills throughout their careers. The established mentor-mentee relationship acts as a source of continuous support and encouragement, crucial for recruits navigating the often-demanding realities of the fire service.

Instructors should also actively promote continuous learning and professional development. Encouraging recruits to pursue further education, attend conferences, and participate in advanced training opportunities underscores the importance of lifelong learning in the fire service. This approach helps recruits see firefighting not as a static career path but as a dynamic field with ongoing opportunities for growth and advancement. By fostering a commitment to continuous learning, instructors are equipping recruits with the tools and motivation to excel in their chosen profession and adapt to the ever-evolving challenges of the fire service. This approach is instrumental in transforming recruits into highly skilled, adaptable professionals who constantly strive for excellence.

Another effective strategy is to emphasize the importance of community engagement. Instructors can arrange visits to local schools, community events, and outreach programs, providing recruits with opportunities to interact with the public and showcase the positive aspects of the fire service. Such interactions build bridges between the fire department and the community it serves. The positive feedback received from community engagement can be highly motivating for recruits, strengthening their sense of purpose and connection to the community. This interaction enhances the recruits' understanding of their community's needs, which directly influences their operational decisions and fosters a sense of mutual respect.

Beyond technical skills, instructors should cultivate recruits' critical thinking and problem-solving abilities. The ability to assess a situation, make informed decisions, and work effectively under pressure is paramount in firefighting. Instructors can incorporate scenario-based training exercises, simulations, and case studies to challenge recruits' cognitive abilities. These exercises allow recruits to practice decision-making skills in a safe environment, fostering confidence and preparedness for real-world scenarios. Through interactive case studies and realistic simulations, recruits gain valuable experience in applying their theoretical knowledge to practical situations, enhancing their critical thinking and problem-solving capabilities.

Recognizing and celebrating achievements is a crucial element in fostering a sense of accomplishment and pride among recruits. Acknowledging individual and team successes, no matter how small, encourages continued effort and motivates recruits to strive for excellence. This positive reinforcement strengthens their confidence and reinforces their commitment to the profession. Public recognition through awards, ceremonies, or departmental newsletters serves as powerful motivation, fostering a positive and supportive environment.

Furthermore, instructors can create a positive and supportive learning environment by establishing open lines of communication and fostering a culture of respect and trust. Encouraging recruits to ask questions, express concerns, and participate actively in discussions promotes a learning culture that is both engaging and productive. Creating a respectful learning environment, where feedback is given constructively and openly, is crucial for developing the recruits' confidence and self-esteem. By adopting such an approach, instructors foster a team environment where feedback is seen as a tool for improvement, promoting growth and encouraging active participation.

In summary, inspiring a passion for the fire service involves a multifaceted approach that goes beyond technical training. It requires instructors to be not just educators but also mentors, storytellers, and motivators. By creating a positive, supportive, and engaging learning environment, fostering a sense of camaraderie and community, promoting continuous learning, and recognizing achievements, instructors can ignite a lasting passion for the profession within their recruits, shaping them into dedicated and highly skilled firefighters who are committed to serving their communities. The investment in fostering this passion yields significant returns, cultivating future leaders in the fire service and ensuring the continued success and safety of the profession. This holistic approach to training ensures the next generation of firefighters not only possesses the necessary skills but also possesses the unwavering commitment and passion to face the challenges inherent in the profession. The lasting impact of an inspiring instructor can shape the career trajectory of many firefighters and ensure that the spirit of service and dedication thrives in the years to come. Therefore, the role of the instructor is not just to teach, but to inspire, shaping the future of the fire service one recruit at a time.

Mentoring and guiding recruits through the inherent challenges of fire service training is paramount to their success and overall well-being. The transition from civilian life to the rigorous demands of a firefighter's career can be overwhelming, requiring a significant shift in mindset and lifestyle. Instructors must recognize this and provide the necessary support to navigate this transition effectively. This support extends beyond technical instruction; it necessitates a genuine commitment to the recruits' personal and professional growth.

One crucial aspect of this support is the establishment of a robust mentoring program. Pairing experienced firefighters with new recruits offers invaluable guidance and personalized support. These mentors serve as role models, not only demonstrating the practical skills of the profession but also sharing their experiences, offering advice on navigating the unique challenges of the job, and fostering a sense of camaraderie and belonging within the department. The mentoring relationship should be built on trust and mutual respect, allowing recruits to openly discuss their concerns and seek guidance without fear of judgment.

Effective mentoring goes beyond simply answering questions; it involves actively listening to the recruit's concerns, understanding their individual learning styles and adapting guidance accordingly. This might involve adjusting training methodologies to better suit the recruit's needs or providing additional support in areas where they are struggling. Mentors should be adept at identifying potential issues before they escalate, offering preventative measures and strategies for success. This proactive approach is vital in preventing burnout and fostering a sense of resilience within the recruit.

Furthermore, the mentoring relationship should extend beyond the immediate training period. Mentors should act as long-term sources of support, providing ongoing guidance and encouragement throughout the recruits' careers. This continuous mentorship fosters a strong sense of loyalty and commitment to the department, ensuring that recruits feel valued and supported throughout their professional journey. Regular check-ins, informal discussions, and opportunities for mentorship to evolve beyond a formal structure are essential to maintaining a strong and supportive relationship.

The challenges faced by recruits are not solely limited to the technical aspects of firefighting. The mental and emotional toll of the job is significant, and instructors must acknowledge and address these aspects proactively. Stress management techniques, mental health awareness, and access to support services are crucial components of a comprehensive training program. Mentors can play a key role in this aspect, providing guidance and support to recruits who may be struggling with the pressures of the job. This might involve referring recruits to appropriate resources, such as counseling services or peer support groups, or simply providing a listening ear and offering words of encouragement.

The integration of stress management and mental wellness into the training curriculum itself is also crucial. Instructors can incorporate techniques such as mindfulness exercises, stress-reduction strategies, and discussions on resilience into the training schedule. This proactive approach aims to equip recruits with the tools they need to manage the inherent stresses of the profession from the outset, fostering both mental and physical well-being. This proactive approach is particularly crucial given the high stress levels associated with emergency response situations and the emotional weight of witnessing traumatic events.

Addressing the physical demands of firefighting is equally important. The rigorous physical training required to become a firefighter can be demanding, requiring recruits to push their physical and mental limits. Mentors and instructors should carefully monitor recruits' physical progress, providing guidance on proper training techniques, injury prevention, and nutrition. Open communication regarding physical limitations or concerns is essential. Creating a supportive and understanding environment ensures recruits feel comfortable voicing their physical limitations without fear of judgment, facilitating an adaptive training approach.

Moreover, the importance of proper nutrition and recovery cannot be overstated. Mentors should emphasize the significance of maintaining a healthy diet and adequate rest to optimize physical performance and prevent injuries. Educating recruits on the importance of sleep, hydration, and proper nutrition is essential for building resilience and maintaining overall well-being throughout their training and subsequent careers. This holistic approach ensures recruits' physical capacity matches the demands of the profession while prioritizing their overall health.

Beyond the physical and mental aspects, recruits often grapple with social and emotional adjustments. The fire service is a close-knit community, and forming strong relationships with fellow recruits and experienced firefighters is crucial for success. Mentors can assist recruits in navigating the social dynamics of the firehouse, helping them build positive relationships and integrate into the team. This fostering of camaraderie translates into stronger teamwork during emergencies and a more supportive and positive work environment. A strong sense of camaraderie is essential to mitigating stress and maintaining morale.

Creating a positive learning environment is critical for success. This means fostering a culture of open communication, mutual respect, and a willingness to learn from mistakes. Instructors should create opportunities for recruits to ask questions, express concerns, and provide feedback without fear of retribution. This open environment encourages active participation and enhances learning. Providing constructive feedback and promoting a culture of continuous improvement is paramount in ensuring recruits reach their full potential. Such an environment fosters confidence and empowers recruits to become active contributors to their team.

Finally, regular feedback and evaluation are essential throughout the training process. Mentors and instructors should provide regular feedback to recruits on their progress, both positive and constructive, highlighting areas of strength and areas for improvement. This consistent feedback loop ensures that recruits are aware of their progress and are able to make necessary adjustments. The feedback mechanism should be collaborative, focusing on improvement rather than judgment, ensuring recruits feel supported and motivated to continue their development. The goal is to foster continuous growth and a lifelong commitment to learning and improvement within the profession. A balanced and positive feedback mechanism is crucial in shaping recruits' confidence and overall success in the demanding environment of the fire service. This holistic approach, encompassing physical, mental, social, and professional aspects, ensures that recruits not only develop the necessary skills but also possess the resilience and well-being to thrive in this challenging but rewarding profession.

Building upon the foundation of individual mentorship and holistic well-being, fostering a culture of teamwork and collaboration is crucial for shaping successful and resilient firefighters. The fire service inherently relies on coordinated action, quick decision-making under pressure, and unwavering trust among team members. These attributes are not innate; they are cultivated through deliberate instruction and the creation of a supportive learning environment that emphasizes collective success. The instructor's role in this process transcends the delivery of technical skills; it involves actively shaping the social fabric of the recruit class, fostering a sense of camaraderie and shared responsibility.

One effective strategy is integrating team-based learning activities into the training curriculum. Moving beyond individual skill assessments, instructors should design exercises that require recruits to work together to solve problems, overcome obstacles, and achieve common goals. These activities can range from simulated emergency scenarios—involving realistic props and challenges—to collaborative problem-solving exercises that require critical thinking and strategic planning. For instance, a scenario might involve a simulated building fire where recruits must coordinate their efforts to locate and rescue victims, while simultaneously managing hose lines and other equipment. The instructor can observe and evaluate not only the individual performance of each recruit but also the effectiveness of their teamwork, communication, and overall strategic approach.

The effectiveness of these team exercises is amplified by incorporating debriefing sessions afterward. These sessions provide a structured environment for recruits to reflect on their performance, discuss their successes and challenges, and learn from their mistakes. The focus should be on constructive feedback and identifying areas for improvement, not assigning blame. The instructor's role here is to facilitate a productive dialogue, encouraging recruits to articulate their experiences and perspectives, identify lessons learned, and collectively develop strategies for enhanced future performance. Debriefing should promote a culture of open communication where mistakes are viewed as learning opportunities, rather than failures.

Beyond simulated scenarios, real-world applications offer invaluable learning experiences. Whenever feasible and safe, incorporating recruits into actual department activities—under close supervision of experienced personnel, of course—provides a tangible understanding of teamwork dynamics in practical contexts. Assisting in training exercises for veteran firefighters, participating in community outreach programs, or even engaging in simple tasks like equipment maintenance and cleaning, all provide opportunities to build camaraderie and reinforce the value of collaboration. These experiences provide a sense of ownership and build confidence, creating a deeper connection to the team and a better understanding of the broader mission of the department.

Furthermore, promoting a culture of respect and inclusivity is paramount. The fire service is becoming increasingly diverse, and instructors must actively cultivate an environment where all recruits feel valued, respected, and empowered to contribute their unique perspectives and skills. This requires a conscious effort to address potential biases, foster open communication about differing backgrounds and experiences, and provide avenues for conflict resolution. The creation of a culture that values diverse experiences and perspectives not only improves team dynamics but also strengthens the team's overall capacity to handle complex situations. A heterogeneous team brings a breadth of knowledge and problem-solving skills that are invaluable in the diverse environments firefighters operate within.

To further strengthen collaborative efforts, instructors should encourage peer-to-peer learning. This involves creating opportunities for recruits to teach and learn from each other. This can be achieved through techniques such as peer instruction, where recruits work in pairs or small groups to explain concepts and solve problems to one another. This not only reinforces their own understanding but also develops their communication and teaching skills. Moreover, this approach can reveal individual strengths and weaknesses more effectively than traditional instructor-led methods. By working collaboratively, recruits identify areas where they excel and areas requiring further development, creating a dynamic and mutually beneficial learning environment.

The use of technology can also enhance collaborative learning. Online platforms and collaborative software can facilitate communication, knowledge sharing, and project management among recruits, even outside of formal training sessions. These platforms provide a space for peer support, discussion, and the exchange of information and resources. This is especially pertinent considering the prevalence of online learning among the current generation of recruits, who are accustomed to digitally mediated communication and interaction. Utilizing such technology not only enhances the learning experience but also mirrors the collaborative nature of modern communication within the fire service.

A crucial aspect of fostering teamwork is promoting effective communication skills. Clear, concise, and unambiguous communication is paramount in emergency situations, and it is essential that recruits develop these skills early on. Instructors should dedicate time to explicit communication training, which can incorporate role-playing exercises, simulations, and scenario-based discussions, focusing on effective radio communication, nonverbal cues, and the importance of active listening. Effective communication is not simply about conveying information; it is about ensuring that information is received and understood correctly, a crucial element for successful teamwork. This training should also emphasize the importance of feedback mechanisms within the team.

The importance of building trust among team members should also be addressed. Trust is the bedrock of effective teamwork, providing the confidence needed for members to rely on each other in high-stress situations. Building trust requires fostering open communication, mutual respect, and the creation of a supportive environment where recruits feel comfortable expressing their opinions and concerns without fear of judgment. Trust-building exercises, focusing on vulnerability and reliance on others, can be implemented throughout the training. These exercises aim to cultivate mutual support and dependence within the team.

Finally, the instructor's role extends to facilitating a culture of continuous learning and improvement. Firefighting is a constantly evolving field, and it is critical that firefighters remain current with best practices and technological advancements. Instructors can promote this by encouraging participation in professional development opportunities, fostering a culture of peer review and self-assessment, and creating an environment where feedback is valued and embraced as a means of growth. The emphasis should always be on continuous improvement, both individually and collectively. This commitment to ongoing development extends beyond the initial training period and becomes a hallmark of a highly effective and adaptive fire service team. Through a multifaceted approach that combines interactive training, technology, and a dedication to ongoing professional development, instructors can cultivate a robust culture of teamwork and collaboration, ensuring the future firefighters are not only highly skilled but also effective, resilient, and highly capable team members.

Building confidence and self-efficacy is paramount in shaping successful firefighters. Recruits entering the fire service often face significant challenges: intense physical demands, exposure to traumatic events, and the constant pressure of life-or-death situations. Equipping them with the psychological resilience to navigate these challenges is as crucial as teaching them technical skills. This involves fostering a growth mindset, promoting self-belief, and providing opportunities for mastery experiences.

One effective strategy is to focus on incremental progress and celebrate small victories. Instead of overwhelming recruits with the vastness of the training curriculum, instructors should break down the learning process into smaller, manageable steps. Each successfully completed step, no matter how small, should be acknowledged and celebrated. This approach builds momentum, creates a sense of accomplishment, and gradually builds confidence. For example, mastering a specific knot, successfully completing a challenging physical training exercise, or correctly executing a rescue technique are all worthy of praise and recognition. This positive reinforcement establishes a pattern of success, counteracting any feelings of inadequacy or self-doubt.

Regular, constructive feedback is essential. This should go beyond simply identifying errors; it should focus on strengths and areas for improvement, emphasizing the recruit's potential for growth. Feedback should be specific, actionable, and delivered in a supportive and encouraging manner. Instead of saying, "Your hose handling was sloppy," a more effective approach would be: "I noticed you struggled slightly with the hose advancements during the drill. Let's work on your grip and technique. Try focusing on maintaining a firm but relaxed grip, and we'll practice some controlled advancements." This approach reframes setbacks as opportunities for learning and improvement.

Moreover, the instructor's language plays a significant role in shaping recruit confidence. Using empowering language, focusing on capabilities rather than limitations, is crucial. Phrases such as, "You can do this," "I have confidence in your abilities," and "Let's work together to overcome this challenge," create a positive and supportive learning environment. In contrast, phrases like, "You're not strong enough," or "You're not cut out for this," can be devastating to a recruit's morale and self-belief. A compassionate and understanding instructor can make all the difference in building a recruit's confidence.

Creating opportunities for mastery experiences is also crucial. These are experiences where recruits can demonstrate their competence and feel a sense of

accomplishment. This could involve mastering a specific skill, successfully completing a challenging exercise, or excelling in a simulated emergency scenario. These successes are invaluable in building self-efficacy, reinforcing the belief that recruits are capable and competent. The instructor's role here is to carefully design training scenarios that allow recruits to progressively demonstrate their mastery, providing ample opportunities for success while gradually increasing the complexity of the challenges.

Role-playing exercises can simulate real-world scenarios and provide a safe space for recruits to practice their skills and build confidence. These exercises allow recruits to practice communication, decision-making, and problem-solving in a low-stakes environment. For instance, a scenario could involve a simulated house fire, requiring recruits to communicate effectively with dispatch, navigate a smoky environment, and rescue victims. The instructor can provide guidance and feedback throughout the exercise, assisting recruits in developing their skills and building their confidence in their ability to handle challenging situations.

Furthermore, incorporating self-assessment into the training process encourages self-reflection and self-evaluation. Regular self-assessments help recruits identify their strengths and weaknesses, track their progress, and set goals for improvement. This process empowers recruits to take ownership of their learning, fostering a sense of independence and self-reliance. These self-assessments can be integrated into the debriefing sessions following practical exercises, allowing recruits to compare their own self-evaluation with the instructor's feedback. This fosters a more comprehensive understanding of their performance and promotes self-awareness.

Another important aspect is building resilience. Firefighters routinely face high-stress situations, and the ability to bounce back from setbacks is crucial. Instructors can help build resilience by modeling positive coping mechanisms, providing opportunities for stress management techniques (such as mindfulness or breathing exercises), and emphasizing the importance of seeking support when needed. The training environment should encourage open communication about stress, challenges, and emotional well-being.

Mentorship programs can also play a significant role. Pairing recruits with experienced firefighters provides them with personalized guidance, support, and encouragement. Mentors can serve as role models, offering advice, sharing their experiences, and providing a sense of belonging. This personalized attention can be particularly beneficial to recruits who may be struggling with self-doubt or lack of confidence. The mentor's role extends beyond technical skills; it encompasses personal growth, building resilience, and fostering a sense of belonging within the fire service community.

Finally, the entire training environment should promote a culture of psychological safety. This means creating a space where recruits feel comfortable taking risks, making mistakes, and seeking help without fear of judgment or reprisal. This environment allows recruits to freely express their concerns, ask questions, and seek clarification without fear of negative consequences. This supportive atmosphere is instrumental in fostering both confidence and trust, leading to a more productive and effective learning experience. Open communication, active listening, and constructive feedback are all key components in establishing this essential culture. By focusing on these multifaceted strategies, instructors can effectively build self-confidence and self-efficacy in their recruits, ensuring they are not only technically proficient but also psychologically resilient, prepared to face the demands of their demanding profession. This holistic approach to training results in firefighters who are confident, competent, and capable of performing their duties effectively and safely.

The impact of a fire service instructor extends far beyond the immediate training period. The lessons learned, the skills acquired, and perhaps most importantly, the values instilled, shape not only the individual firefighter but the entire fire service culture for years to come. A single instructor can inadvertently influence hundreds, even thousands, of firefighters throughout their careers through the ripple effect of their teaching and mentorship. Consider the impact of an instructor who teaches effective communication techniques: Their students will then implement those skills on the job, influencing their colleagues, superiors, and the public they serve. Effective communication is not merely a technical skill; it is a cornerstone of teamwork, safety, and public relations, impacting the entire fire service ecosystem.

This lasting influence underscores the critical need for high-quality instructor training. Investing in comprehensive instructor development programs is not just an expense; it is a strategic investment in the future of the fire service. These programs should focus not only on the technical aspects of firefighting but also on effective pedagogical techniques, adult learning principles, and the importance of fostering a positive and supportive learning environment. A well-trained instructor understands how to adapt their teaching style to suit the diverse learning needs of their students, employing a variety of methods to maximize engagement and retention. They recognize that learning is not a passive process; it's an active, iterative experience that requires a blend of theoretical instruction, practical exercises, and opportunities for feedback and reflection.

The modern fire service recruit comes from a diverse range of backgrounds and experiences. Some may have prior military or emergency medical services experience, others may have no prior experience at all. Some may thrive in traditional lecture-based settings, while others prefer hands-on learning and active participation. A skilled instructor is adept at recognizing and catering to these diverse learning styles. They understand that "one-size-fits-all" approach is outdated and ineffective. Rather than a rigid, standardized curriculum, a modern instructor employs flexible, adaptable methods, employing a variety of teaching strategies—from interactive simulations to problem-based learning to project-based learning—to keep their students engaged and challenged.

Furthermore, the instructor's role transcends the purely technical. They serve as mentors, role models, and leaders, shaping not just the skills but the character of future firefighters. They instill the values of courage, teamwork, compassion, and integrity—values that are crucial not only in responding to emergencies but also in navigating the complex dynamics of the fire service workplace. A compassionate and understanding instructor can make a significant difference in fostering a positive and supportive team dynamic. Their ability to create a psychologically safe learning environment is critical, particularly given the high-stress nature of the fire service profession. Recruits must feel comfortable expressing concerns, asking questions, and seeking clarification without fear of judgment or reprisal. This supportive atmosphere fosters open communication, enhances team cohesion, and promotes learning effectiveness.

The instructor's influence extends to the development of problem-solving skills. Firefighting is not simply a collection of techniques; it requires critical thinking, adaptability, and effective decision-making under pressure. Experienced instructors design training scenarios that challenge recruits to think critically, analyze situations, and develop creative solutions. These scenarios might involve simulated emergency response, where recruits must apply their technical skills and knowledge in a realistic context, or problem-solving exercises designed to test their ability to handle unexpected challenges. This type of training goes beyond rote memorization; it cultivates a more resilient and resourceful firefighter.

Moreover, the instructor's role in fostering continuous professional development is invaluable. The fire service is a constantly evolving field, with new technologies, techniques, and challenges emerging regularly. Effective instructors don't simply deliver information; they instill a lifelong commitment to learning. They encourage their students to pursue further training and education, to remain abreast of the latest developments, and to engage in continuous self-improvement. This commitment to continuous learning ensures that firefighters remain competent, adaptable, and well-equipped to handle the challenges of their profession throughout their careers. This commitment is not only conveyed through words but also through modeling lifelong learning themselves—staying updated on advancements, participating in professional development, and attending relevant conferences.

The instructor's influence extends beyond the classroom or training yard. They contribute to the creation of a positive and supportive team culture. Their attitudes, behavior, and leadership style directly influence the overall atmosphere within the department. A supportive and understanding instructor helps create a climate where teamwork and mutual respect are valued. This positive environment fosters camaraderie, enhances team performance, and contributes to a more robust and effective fire service organization. This culture of collaboration is particularly important in the high-pressure environment of the fire service, where teamwork and trust are paramount to safety and success.

Furthermore, the instructor plays a pivotal role in shaping the future of safety and preventative measures. By imparting not only the technical skills of firefighting but also the importance of fire prevention, hazard mitigation, and community outreach, instructors contribute to a larger movement aimed at reducing fire incidents and improving overall public safety. This contribution is vital, as it demonstrates the far-reaching impact of fire service training, extending beyond emergency response to a proactive approach to community well-being. The focus here extends to educating the public on fire safety through presentations, workshops, and community events. Such involvement creates a stronger relationship between the fire service and the community it protects.

Finally, the lasting impact of instructors is immeasurable. Their influence resonates not only through the firefighters they train but also through the generations of firefighters who are subsequently trained by those initial students. This creates a chain of positive influence, with each generation of instructors building upon the knowledge, skills, and values instilled by their predecessors. This continuing legacy ensures that the fire service upholds its commitment to excellence, safety, and community service for generations to come. The commitment to training excellence is therefore not just a short-term investment; it is a strategic long-term strategy that secures the future of the fire service. It is an investment in the lives saved, the communities protected, and the future of a profession built on courage, skill, and unwavering dedication. This legacy of excellence—cultivated and nurtured by dedicated instructors—is the true testament to the profound and lasting impact of exceptional fire service instruction.

Chapter 8: Technology in Fire Service Training

The integration of technology into fire service training is rapidly evolving, and one of the most exciting developments is the increasing use of virtual reality (VR) and simulation training. These technologies offer unprecedented opportunities to enhance practical skills, improve safety, and create a more engaging and effective learning environment for recruits. Traditional training methods, while valuable, often rely on limited real-world scenarios and can be costly and logistically challenging. VR and simulation training offer a cost-effective and safe alternative that addresses these limitations, providing a realistic and repeatable environment for honing critical skills.

The immersive nature of VR allows trainees to experience realistic fire scenarios without the inherent risks of real-world training exercises. Imagine a recruit navigating a simulated burning building, encountering smoke-filled hallways, and encountering challenges such as zero visibility and obstructed pathways. Through VR, they can practice search and rescue techniques, master hose deployment and advancement, and learn effective communication protocols all within a controlled, virtual environment. This repetitive practice, achievable within a VR setting, is invaluable, allowing for skill refinement and the development of muscle memory critical to effective performance under pressure.

Unlike traditional training, VR allows for multiple scenarios to be crafted and delivered. This flexibility ensures a variety of training experiences, ranging from simple scenarios to complex, multi-faceted simulations that integrate several aspects of firefighting. Recruits can learn to react to unexpected changes, handle equipment malfunctions, and address evolving situations, thus promoting adaptability and problem-solving skills—highly valued traits in emergency response situations. The ability to adjust the difficulty and complexity of the simulation, based on the trainee's skill level, allows for personalized training pathways. This ensures trainees are challenged appropriately and helps to avoid overwhelming beginners with overly complex tasks.

Furthermore, VR simulations offer a risk-free environment to practice potentially dangerous maneuvers. Trainees can make mistakes without fear of injury or property damage. They can experiment with different techniques, learn from their errors, and refine their approach without real-world consequences. This fosters a culture of experimentation and learning, encouraging recruits to take calculated risks within a safety net. This feature is particularly valuable when training for high-stakes situations, such as high-angle rescue or confined-space operations.

The data generated by VR simulations provides valuable insights into trainee performance. The system can track movements, decisions, and response times, providing instructors with objective feedback and identifying areas requiring additional attention. This data-driven approach to training ensures that each recruit receives individualized instruction tailored to their specific needs and progress. It allows for accurate assessment of skills, timely intervention, and a precise focus on areas requiring improvement, leading to a more efficient training process and improved overall proficiency.

Beyond the practical skills training, VR simulations can also effectively address critical decision-making and leadership roles within the fire service. Simulations can replicate complex incidents where decision-making under extreme pressure is paramount. This allows recruits to practice assigning tasks, coordinating teams, and managing resources in a safe and controlled setting. The feedback system integrated into the VR training provides immediate and constructive criticism, reinforcing both correct decision-making and highlighting areas requiring improved leadership.

Moreover, VR can be utilized to simulate challenging interpersonal scenarios encountered during emergency responses and within the firehouse. It allows for the practice of effective communication, conflict resolution, and teamwork in high-pressure environments. This type of training goes beyond the technical aspects of firefighting, addressing the equally critical soft skills necessary for successful teamwork and positive interpersonal dynamics. Training in these situations builds confidence and competence in navigating potentially tense situations, ensuring smooth collaboration during real emergency scenarios.

The cost-effectiveness of VR and simulation training should also be considered. While the initial investment in VR technology may seem significant, the long-term cost savings can be substantial. Traditional training often requires large-scale props, extensive personnel, and potentially costly site preparation. VR eliminates these factors, resulting in significant cost savings over the long term. Furthermore, the repetitive nature of VR allows for consistent and efficient training, increasing the overall return on investment. It also reduces the risk of damage to expensive training equipment, further reducing operational costs.

The implementation of VR and simulation training requires careful planning and execution. The selection of appropriate software and hardware is crucial, ensuring compatibility with training objectives and the budget constraints of the fire department. Furthermore, instructor training is vital. Instructors must be trained in the use of VR technology and the appropriate pedagogical approaches for maximizing its effectiveness. They need to be equipped to analyze the data generated by the simulations and provide meaningful feedback to the trainees. This requires investment in instructor development, ensuring that they are capable of effectively utilizing this new technology to optimize the training experience.

The success of VR training also relies on the engagement and buy-in from trainees. The technology must be user-friendly, intuitive, and engaging to maintain the interest and attention of the recruits. Instructors need to foster a positive and supportive learning environment, encouraging experimentation and learning from mistakes. This ensures that trainees fully embrace the VR technology as a powerful tool for enhancing their skills and building their confidence. Regular feedback and a clear understanding of the learning objectives are also critical to maintaining the motivation and engagement of trainees.

Beyond the immediate benefits of enhanced training, VR and simulation technology can be leveraged for ongoing professional development. It is a dynamic platform that can be updated with new techniques, evolving fire safety regulations, and new firefighting equipment. This ensures firefighters are kept current with the latest developments, providing continuous professional development. This continuous updating of the simulation software allows for ongoing refinement and improvement of the training program, ensuring its relevance and effectiveness. This proactive approach to professional development helps reduce the reliance on costly and time-consuming refresher courses, streamlining the ongoing training requirements.

The integration of VR and simulation training marks a significant advancement in fire service training. Its ability to provide realistic, safe, and effective training opportunities presents an opportunity to improve the skills, safety, and overall performance of firefighters. It's a strategic investment that delivers enhanced training outcomes, reduces risks, and optimizes resource utilization. While challenges remain in its implementation, the potential benefits of virtual reality in revolutionizing fire service training are clear and compelling, ultimately leading to a better-prepared and safer fire service workforce. The future of fire service training is increasingly technological, and VR is at the forefront of this exciting evolution.

The effectiveness of VR and simulation training, as discussed, underscores the broader shift towards leveraging technology for improved fire service training. This technological revolution extends beyond immersive simulations, encompassing a wide range of interactive learning platforms and online resources that significantly augment traditional training methodologies. These digital tools offer accessible, flexible, and engaging learning experiences, catering to the diverse learning styles prevalent among today's recruits.

One of the key advantages of online learning platforms is their accessibility. Geographic limitations, previously a significant hurdle to consistent and widespread training, are largely eliminated. Fire departments in remote areas, or those with limited access to specialized training facilities, can now tap into a wealth of online resources, ensuring their personnel receive the same high-quality training as their counterparts in more urban settings. This democratization of access to high-quality training materials is particularly significant for smaller departments with limited budgets and resources.

Furthermore, the flexibility offered by online platforms is unparalleled. Recruits can access training materials at their own pace and convenience, allowing for personalized learning experiences tailored to their individual needs and schedules. This asynchronous learning model contrasts sharply with the rigid timetable of traditional classroom-based training, accommodating recruits' diverse commitments and learning preferences. This self-directed learning empowers recruits to focus on areas requiring additional attention, revisiting challenging concepts as needed. This flexibility is particularly beneficial for those who benefit from repeated exposure to the material or prefer a more deliberate approach to learning.

The engagement factor of well-designed online platforms is crucial. Interactive modules, simulations, and gamified learning experiences can significantly enhance the learning process, moving away from passive learning and encouraging active participation. This shift towards active learning is supported by numerous pedagogical studies demonstrating its superior effectiveness compared to traditional lecture-based methods. Engaging content keeps recruits motivated, improving knowledge retention and ensuring a more effective training outcome. For instance, online quizzes, interactive case studies, and virtual fireground scenarios can transform the learning experience from a passive reception of information to an active engagement with the subject matter.

Many online platforms offer a range of features designed to enhance the learning experience. These include interactive exercises, simulations, virtual reality components, and progress tracking tools that provide immediate feedback to the learner. These features create a dynamic and engaging learning environment, reinforcing learning and improving knowledge retention. Progress tracking tools allow both the recruit and the instructor to monitor progress, identify areas needing improvement, and provide targeted feedback. This individualized approach to learning addresses the diverse needs of recruits, ensuring that everyone receives the support they need to succeed.

The availability of a diverse range of online resources is another significant advantage. Numerous websites, educational platforms, and professional organizations offer a vast library of training materials, encompassing various aspects of fire service operations. This includes videos, presentations, interactive simulations, and downloadable documents covering topics ranging from basic firefighting techniques to advanced emergency medical services protocols. This extensive resource base ensures a comprehensive and up-to-date training program. Moreover, access to this broad range of resources allows for greater customization of training programs, catering to the specific needs of individual departments and their personnel.

The integration of online learning platforms into existing training programs should be carefully planned and implemented. It's crucial to select platforms that align with the department's learning objectives, budget, and technological infrastructure. Instructors should be thoroughly trained on how to effectively utilize the platform's features and incorporate them into their teaching strategies. This ensures seamless integration and maximizes the benefits of online learning. Providing adequate support to recruits as they navigate the online platform is also essential, addressing any technical challenges or learning difficulties they encounter. This supportive approach minimizes frustration and enhances the overall learning experience.

Effective online learning relies on a strong foundation of pedagogical principles. While the technology facilitates the learning process, effective instruction remains paramount. The use of diverse teaching methods, such as blended learning which combines online and in-person training, is particularly effective. This approach allows for a balance between the flexibility and accessibility of online learning and the hands-on learning opportunities provided by in-person training. It ensures a holistic and engaging learning experience, catering to the diverse learning styles and preferences of recruits.

The integration of technology into fire service training extends beyond the use of specific platforms and resources; it encompasses a shift in pedagogical approaches. The move towards personalized, self-directed learning requires a change in instructional methodology. Instructors need to adopt a more facilitative role, guiding and supporting recruits as they navigate the learning process rather than simply delivering lectures. This learner-centric approach empowers recruits to take ownership of their learning, leading to enhanced knowledge retention and improved engagement. This also emphasizes the importance of regular feedback, ensuring that recruits receive timely support and guidance throughout their training.

Furthermore, continuous evaluation and improvement are integral aspects of integrating online learning platforms into fire service training programs. Regular assessments of platform effectiveness, feedback from both instructors and recruits, and the ongoing evaluation of learning outcomes are essential. This continuous improvement cycle ensures that the chosen platforms remain relevant, effective, and aligned with the evolving needs of the fire service. Data analysis of trainee performance on online modules provides valuable insights, informing improvements in both the training content and the delivery methodology.

The ongoing development of new technologies and platforms presents both opportunities and challenges. Fire service training officers must stay abreast of technological advancements, exploring new tools and methods that can enhance the effectiveness of their training programs. This requires ongoing professional development for instructors, equipping them with the knowledge and skills to utilize new technologies effectively. The adoption of new technologies should always be informed by a solid understanding of pedagogical principles, ensuring that technology complements, rather than substitutes for, effective instruction.

In conclusion, the integration of interactive learning platforms and online resources into fire service training represents a significant advancement in the field. These technologies offer unparalleled accessibility, flexibility, and engagement, fostering a more effective and efficient learning experience for recruits. However, successful implementation requires careful planning, instructor training, and a commitment to continuous evaluation and improvement. By embracing technology and adapting pedagogical approaches, fire service training can be transformed into a more dynamic, engaging, and effective process, ultimately leading to a better-prepared and more capable fire service workforce. The focus must remain on integrating technology to enhance, not replace, the core principles of effective fire service training and ensuring the safety and proficiency of our firefighters. The future of firefighter training is not just about the 'how' but also—crucially—the 'why,' and technology empowers us to deliver both with increased effectiveness.

The integration of technology into fire service training, as discussed, offers numerous advantages, but its true potential is unlocked through the strategic application of data analytics. By systematically collecting, analyzing, and interpreting data related to training outcomes, we can move beyond anecdotal observations and gain a precise understanding of what works, what doesn't, and where improvements are needed. This data-driven approach allows for the continuous optimization of training programs, ensuring they remain effective, efficient, and aligned with the evolving needs of the fire service.

One of the primary benefits of using data analytics is the ability to accurately measure training effectiveness. Traditional methods of assessing training outcomes often rely on subjective evaluations, such as instructor observations or informal feedback from recruits. While these methods provide valuable insights, they lack the objectivity and quantifiable metrics that data analytics provides. By tracking key performance indicators (KPIs) such as test scores, simulation performance, practical skills assessments, and even recruit feedback collected through online surveys, we can obtain a precise and comprehensive measure of training effectiveness. This detailed data allows for a clear understanding of which aspects of the training program are most successful and which require attention.

For example, a fire department might utilize a learning management system (LMS) that tracks the time spent by recruits on various modules, their performance on quizzes and simulations, and the number of attempts needed to successfully complete specific exercises. This data can reveal patterns indicating areas of difficulty or confusion for recruits. Are recruits struggling with a particular concept? Is a certain training module too complex or too simple? By analyzing this data, instructors can identify areas needing improvement or clarification, potentially tailoring their teaching methods or updating the training materials to address specific challenges.

Furthermore, data analytics allows for the identification of learning gaps and areas where recruits require additional support. By analyzing performance data across different modules, instructors can pinpoint specific skills or concepts where recruits are struggling. This information can then be used to develop targeted interventions, such as supplemental training sessions, additional practice exercises, or personalized coaching. This personalized approach to training addresses the diverse needs of recruits, ensuring that everyone receives the support they need to succeed. This contrasts sharply with traditional approaches where learning gaps might go unnoticed until they manifest in critical situations during actual emergency responses.

Data analytics also extends beyond the individual recruit level. It can be used to evaluate the effectiveness of various training methods and approaches. For instance, a department might compare the performance of recruits trained using traditional methods with those trained using immersive VR simulations. By analyzing the data, they can determine which approach leads to better knowledge retention and improved practical skills. This evidence-based approach informs future training decisions, ensuring that the department employs the most effective techniques. Similarly, the effectiveness of different teaching styles, the impact of various online platforms, and the usefulness of different learning materials can be objectively assessed and improved.

The integration of data analytics into fire service training requires the use of appropriate technologies and tools. Learning management systems (LMS) are a crucial component, providing a centralized platform for tracking recruit progress and performance. These systems typically include features such as automated assessments, progress tracking, and personalized feedback mechanisms. Furthermore, the use of data visualization tools can make complex data sets more accessible and understandable for instructors, providing a clear picture of training effectiveness. These tools can generate charts, graphs, and other visual representations that highlight trends, patterns, and areas needing improvement.

The collection and analysis of training data should always be conducted ethically and responsibly. Data privacy is paramount, and all data collection and usage practices must comply with relevant regulations and ethical guidelines. Recruit data should be anonymized whenever possible, and all personal information should be protected. Transparency is essential, and recruits should be informed about how their data is being used. Building trust with recruits through open communication about data usage is crucial for promoting the successful integration of data analytics into training programs.

Beyond the LMS, other data sources can significantly enhance the overall analysis. Feedback surveys can provide valuable insights into the recruits' perceptions of the training program, helping to identify areas needing improvement or adjustments to better suit their learning styles. Incident reports can inform the curriculum, ensuring that training

147.

adequately prepares firefighters for real-world scenarios. This data, when combined with performance data from the LMS, provides a more holistic understanding of training effectiveness and its impact on real-world preparedness.

The use of predictive analytics is also becoming increasingly relevant in fire service training. By analyzing historical data, it's possible to identify risk factors that might predict future performance or identify potential areas where recruits might struggle. This information can be used to implement proactive measures to mitigate these risks and provide targeted support to those at risk. This approach emphasizes a preventative approach to training, ensuring recruits develop the necessary skills and competencies to perform effectively in high-pressure situations.

However, it is crucial to acknowledge the limitations of data analytics. Data analysis is only as good as the data it's based on. Inaccurate or incomplete data can lead to misleading conclusions. It is imperative to ensure the quality and reliability of data collection methods. Additionally, data analysis alone cannot replace the judgment and experience of skilled instructors. While data can inform decision-making, it should be used to supplement, not replace, the expertise of seasoned professionals in the fire service. The human element in training remains irreplaceable.

Furthermore, the interpretation of data requires careful consideration. While data can highlight trends and patterns, it doesn't always provide a complete picture. Instructors need to be able to critically evaluate the data, considering contextual factors and potential biases. For example, a low test score on a particular module might not always indicate a lack of understanding; it could be due to a poorly designed test or other external factors. Instructors must use their professional judgment to interpret the data in the proper context.

The ongoing evolution of data analytics and technology necessitates continuous professional development for fire service instructors. To effectively utilize data analytics tools and interpret the resulting information, instructors must receive adequate training and support. This professional development should include not just technical skills, but also pedagogical approaches to leverage the data for improved teaching and learning. Keeping abreast of the latest advancements in this field is crucial for maximizing the benefits of data analytics in fire service training.

In conclusion, data analytics is a powerful tool for improving the effectiveness and efficiency of fire service training. By using data to measure outcomes, identify learning gaps, and evaluate different training methods, fire departments can optimize their training programs, ensure recruit preparedness, and ultimately enhance public safety. However, successful implementation requires careful planning, ethical considerations, the development of appropriate technological infrastructure, and a commitment to continuous professional development for instructors. The integration of data-driven approaches into fire service training represents a significant step forward in ensuring the safety and effectiveness of our firefighters. The goal is to use data to enhance, not replace, the crucial human element of effective training and mentoring, allowing us to build a better-prepared, more capable, and safer fire service for the future.

The shift towards mobile learning in the fire service is a natural progression, reflecting the ubiquitous nature of smartphones and tablets in modern life. Recruits, accustomed to accessing information readily and on demand, readily embrace training delivered through mobile devices. This approach not only provides flexibility and convenience but also caters to diverse learning styles and preferences. No longer confined to the classroom or training facility, learning can occur anytime, anywhere – on a lunch break, during downtime at the station, or even during commutes. This accessibility significantly increases the likelihood of consistent engagement and knowledge retention.

Mobile learning platforms offer a vast array of functionalities beyond simple text delivery. Interactive simulations can mimic real-life scenarios, allowing recruits to practice decision-making and skill application in a risk-free environment.

High-quality video demonstrations can showcase proper techniques and procedures, offering visual reinforcement that complements written materials. Quizzes and assessments, integrated directly into the mobile platform, provide immediate feedback, enabling recruits to identify and address knowledge gaps promptly. This immediate feedback loop is critical for reinforcing learning and improving understanding, contributing significantly to enhanced knowledge retention and overall training effectiveness.

Effective mobile learning relies heavily on the careful design and development of the training content. The information needs to be chunked into smaller, easily digestible modules, which leads us to the crucial concept of microlearning. Microlearning focuses on delivering concise, focused learning experiences. Instead of lengthy lectures or modules, training materials are broken down into short, self-contained segments, typically lasting between 2 and 10 minutes. This approach recognizes the limitations of sustained attention spans in a fast-paced world and caters to the way modern learners prefer to absorb information.

The benefits of microlearning are multifaceted. Firstly, it promotes focused learning, improving concentration and comprehension. By focusing on a single, specific concept or skill within a short timeframe, recruits can more easily grasp the information without feeling overwhelmed. Secondly, microlearning enhances knowledge retention due to the shorter, more manageable learning units. The brain processes information more effectively in smaller chunks, increasing the chances of memorization and recall. Thirdly, microlearning fosters a sense of accomplishment and encourages consistent engagement. The rapid completion of short modules provides a sense of progress and encourages recruits to continue with the training. Finally, microlearning enhances flexibility and accessibility, aligning perfectly with the mobile learning paradigm. Short modules can easily be completed in short bursts of time, fitting seamlessly into even the busiest schedules.

When designing microlearning modules, several key principles should be considered. The content should be concise and focused, avoiding unnecessary jargon or complexity. Visual aids, such as images, videos, and interactive elements, can significantly enhance engagement and understanding. Regular quizzes and assessments are crucial to reinforce learning and provide immediate feedback. The overall design should be user-friendly and intuitive, allowing recruits to navigate the modules easily and effectively. A well-designed microlearning module is not just about presenting information; it's about creating an engaging and effective learning experience.

The implementation of mobile learning and microlearning within the fire service requires a strategic approach. It begins with a thorough assessment of existing training needs and learning objectives. This will inform the development of appropriate training content and the selection of an appropriate mobile learning platform. The platform chosen should be user-friendly, compatible with various devices, and capable of integrating with existing systems. Careful consideration should be given to issues of data security and privacy. Training instructors need adequate support and professional development to effectively utilize the chosen platform and deliver training content in an engaging and effective way.

The successful integration of mobile and microlearning requires a commitment to ongoing evaluation and refinement. Regular feedback from instructors and recruits is vital to identify areas for improvement. Data analytics plays a critical role in evaluating the effectiveness of the training modules, including time spent, performance on quizzes, and overall user engagement metrics. This allows for continuous refinement and optimization of the training content and the platform itself, adapting to the ever-evolving needs and preferences of modern recruits.

One practical application of mobile microlearning is in the area of emergency medical services (EMS) training. Short modules focused on specific medical procedures, such as CPR, wound care, or the administration of medication, can be readily delivered through a mobile app. Each module can contain high-quality video demonstrations, interactive simulations, and knowledge checks, reinforcing the learning process. This approach allows recruits to refresh their knowledge and skills at their convenience, ensuring preparedness and competence in a high-pressure environment. This approach also caters to the realities of busy schedules and the need for frequent practice and reinforcement in a time-sensitive field.

Another application involves hazardous materials (Hazmat) response training. Given the complexity of Hazmat incidents and the range of potential hazards, microlearning provides a practical means to deliver crucial information in bite-sized pieces. Each module can focus on a specific aspect of Hazmat response, such as recognizing hazardous materials, understanding safety protocols, or using specialized equipment. Interactive simulations can realistically simulate Hazmat scenarios, allowing recruits to practice decision-making under pressure. This mobile-based approach allows for training on-the-go, supplementing traditional classroom and field exercises.

In the realm of fire suppression techniques, mobile microlearning could effectively reinforce concepts taught in the traditional classroom. Short videos demonstrating proper hose handling, ventilation procedures, or search and rescue techniques can enhance comprehension and retention. Interactive quizzes could reinforce understanding of fire dynamics and safety protocols. This supplementary approach, delivered through a user-friendly mobile app, effectively complements other training methods and ensures continuous reinforcement and improved knowledge retention.

The integration of augmented reality (AR) and virtual reality (VR) further enhances the capabilities of mobile microlearning. AR overlays digital information onto the real world, potentially providing real-time feedback during training exercises. For example, AR could guide recruits through a simulated fire scene, offering instructions and highlighting potential hazards. VR provides immersive simulations of real-world scenarios, allowing recruits to practice their skills in a risk-free environment. These immersive technologies enhance engagement, improve knowledge retention, and provide a more realistic and effective training experience.

However, the implementation of mobile and microlearning also presents certain challenges. The initial investment in developing high-quality mobile learning content and selecting an appropriate platform can be significant. Ensuring equitable access to technology and reliable internet connectivity for all recruits is crucial. There's also a need for appropriate support and training for instructors to effectively utilize this technology. Regular evaluation and refinement of the training content are critical to ensure its effectiveness and alignment with the evolving needs of the fire service. Addressing these challenges proactively ensures the successful integration of mobile and microlearning into fire service training programs. This investment in technology is an investment in the safety and effectiveness of our firefighters, ultimately leading to enhanced public safety.

Augmented reality (AR) offers a transformative potential for fire service training, moving beyond the limitations of traditional methods and leveraging technology to create more immersive and effective learning experiences. Unlike virtual reality (VR), which completely immerses the user in a simulated environment, AR overlays digital information onto the real world, allowing trainees to interact with both the physical and virtual elements simultaneously. This blend of the real and the virtual creates a uniquely powerful training tool.

154.

One of the most compelling applications of AR in fire service training lies in its ability to create interactive simulations of real-world scenarios. Imagine recruits practicing search and rescue techniques in a burning building – not a physically constructed mock-up, but the department's actual training facility, enhanced by AR. Using AR headsets or tablets, recruits could see a digitally projected fire, complete with realistic smoke and flames, obscuring their vision and simulating the challenging conditions of a real fire. The AR system could then overlay pathways, highlighting potential hazards, and providing guidance on safe navigation techniques. Trainees could practice their search patterns, learning to overcome obstacles and prioritize safety while operating within a familiar, yet enhanced, training space.

Furthermore, AR can add layers of information beyond visual cues. The system could display real-time temperature readings, oxygen levels, and the location of trapped victims, providing recruits with crucial data that reinforces the importance of risk assessment and situational awareness. This integration of digital data with the physical environment allows for a much more nuanced and comprehensive understanding of the challenges involved in firefighting. The system could also provide immediate feedback, highlighting correct and incorrect actions, reinforcing best practices, and identifying areas for improvement.

Beyond search and rescue, AR can enhance training in other crucial areas. For example, in hazardous materials (Hazmat) response, AR can transform a training scenario from a simple identification exercise into an immersive experience. Instead of simply pointing to pictures in a manual, trainees could use their AR devices to scan a variety of containers, and the system would immediately overlay critical information about the contents, potential hazards, and appropriate response procedures. This interactive identification process allows recruits to practice crucial decision-making under pressure in a safe, controlled environment. Imagine a scenario where the AR system places trainees in a contaminated area. The system can visually highlight the danger zones, display contamination levels, and guide them through the proper decontamination procedures. This level of interactive engagement provides a level of understanding and retention significantly higher than traditional methods.

AR can also greatly benefit the training of emergency medical services (EMS) personnel within a fire service. AR applications could overlay anatomical models onto real patients (simulated or real, with appropriate permissions and ethical considerations), guiding trainees through procedures like CPR or intravenous insertion with real-time feedback. This dynamic approach allows for practice in a more realistic setting, improving dexterity, precision and critical thinking skills in a risk-free environment. AR could also provide a detailed explanation of the physiological impacts of injury or illness overlaid onto the patient's body, linking visual cues to the underlying medical conditions. This approach helps bridge the gap between theoretical knowledge and practical application.

The application of AR isn't limited to simulations. It can enhance the efficiency and effectiveness of everyday training activities. For instance, AR can overlay instructions and diagrams onto real-world equipment, guiding trainees through the complex operation of various apparatus such as fire pumps, aerial ladders, or specialized rescue equipment. By having digital instructions projected directly onto the equipment itself, the trainees can see exactly how the components fit together, how they operate, and where specific functionalities are located. This removes the need for constant reference to bulky manuals and promotes a more intuitive understanding of the equipment's use. It also allows for hands-on practice with immediate feedback.

Another significant advantage of AR in fire service training is its potential for personalized learning. The system can adapt to individual learning styles and paces, providing customized feedback and challenging trainees at an appropriate level. If a recruit struggles with a particular technique, the AR system can offer additional practice exercises or alternative explanations. This personalized approach caters to the diverse learning needs of each recruit, ultimately leading to a more effective and efficient learning experience.

However, the integration of AR into fire service training presents some challenges. The initial investment in AR hardware and software can be substantial. Departments need to consider the cost of AR headsets, tablets, and the development of high-quality AR applications tailored to their specific needs. Moreover, ensuring that all trainees have access to the necessary technology and reliable internet connectivity is critical for equitable participation. This may require significant investment in infrastructure upgrades.

The effective use of AR also requires adequate training for instructors. They need to be familiar with the technology and understand how to best integrate it into their existing training programs. This may necessitate specialized training sessions or workshops to equip instructors with the skills needed to effectively utilize AR tools. Furthermore, the development of engaging and effective AR applications requires specialized expertise in game design, 3D modeling, and software development. This could involve partnering with external companies or creating internal development teams.

The ongoing maintenance and updates of AR applications are also important considerations. As technology evolves, existing AR applications may need to be updated to ensure compatibility with newer hardware and software. This requires ongoing investment in software maintenance and updates. Regular evaluation of the effectiveness of AR training is crucial. Data analytics can play a vital role in measuring trainee performance, identifying areas for improvement in the AR applications, and ensuring the technology effectively enhances learning outcomes.

Despite these challenges, the potential benefits of AR in fire service training are substantial. By creating more immersive, interactive, and personalized learning experiences, AR can significantly improve the knowledge retention, skills development, and overall preparedness of firefighters. This ultimately contributes to enhanced safety for both firefighters and the public they serve, justifying the investment in this cutting-edge technology. The future of fire service training undoubtedly incorporates innovative technologies, and AR is poised to be a major component of that future. The focus should be on strategic implementation, addressing the challenges proactively, and continuously evaluating its effectiveness to optimize its impact on training programs and improve firefighter preparedness.

Chapter 9: Curriculum Design and Development

Designing a truly engaging and relevant curriculum for fire service recruits requires a deep understanding of adult learning principles and a commitment to moving beyond traditional, lecture-based approaches.

The modern recruit, often shaped by self-directed online learning and accustomed to immediate feedback, demands a more interactive and dynamic learning environment. The emphasis must shift from simply conveying information to fostering a genuine understanding of *why* certain techniques and procedures are crucial, before diving into the *how*. This "Why Before the How" philosophy is central to building a strong foundation of knowledge and developing a passion for the profession.

A key element in achieving this is the careful selection and sequencing of learning objectives. Instead of presenting a long list of skills and techniques, the curriculum should be structured around overarching themes and competencies. For example, rather than focusing solely on individual aspects of fireground operations, the curriculum should emphasize the overarching goal of effective and safe incident management. Within this framework, individual skills such as search and rescue, ventilation, and hose handling can be taught in context, highlighting their contribution to overall situational awareness and safety. This holistic approach helps recruits see the "big picture," understanding how individual skills contribute to the broader objectives of the fire service.

The chosen learning methods should reflect this integrated approach. Traditional lectures, while having a place, should be minimized in favor of interactive workshops, simulations, and hands-on exercises. These methods encourage active participation and allow recruits to apply their knowledge in a safe, controlled environment. For example, a scenario-based training exercise could simulate a residential structure fire, incorporating all aspects of fireground operations—size-up, risk assessment, strategy development, and tactical execution. This integrated approach allows recruits to practice their skills in a realistic context, fostering a deeper understanding of their role within the overall incident management process. This type of integrated approach fosters improved teamwork, communication and decision-making skills.

Furthermore, incorporating real-world case studies and examples is vital. Sharing stories of past incidents, analyzing successful interventions, and examining incidents where errors occurred can provide valuable learning opportunities. These case studies can demonstrate the practical application of skills and techniques, highlighting the consequences of both effective and ineffective actions. This approach not only reinforces the importance of proper procedures but also fosters critical thinking skills, allowing recruits to learn from the experiences of others.

Technology plays a crucial role in enhancing curriculum engagement. We've already explored the transformative potential of augmented reality (AR), but other technologies also have significant value. Virtual reality (VR) simulations can replicate high-risk scenarios, providing trainees with the opportunity to practice decision-making in a safe and controlled environment, without putting themselves or others at risk. Consider a VR simulation of a high-rise fire, where trainees must navigate complex building layouts, contend with challenging atmospheric conditions and make critical decisions under immense pressure. This allows for repeated practice and refinement of skills without the inherent risks of live training exercises.

Interactive online learning platforms offer another avenue for engaging recruits. These platforms can provide tailored learning experiences, adjusting to individual learning styles and pacing. They offer immediate feedback, allowing recruits to assess their understanding and identify areas requiring further study. Furthermore, online platforms can facilitate collaborative learning, fostering peer-to-peer support and knowledge exchange.

However, effective integration of technology requires careful planning and implementation. It's not simply a matter of replacing traditional methods with technology; rather, it's about strategically using technology to enhance the learning experience. Proper training for instructors in the use of these new tools is crucial. Training officers must be comfortable guiding trainees through these new technologies and effectively integrating them into the existing curriculum. This may include specialized training sessions or workshops to ensure instructors can adapt to the new technological tools, understand how best to utilize them within their training, and how to facilitate effective learning experiences.

Assessment is an equally critical component of curriculum design. Evaluation should go beyond traditional written exams, embracing a variety of methods to gauge knowledge retention and skills development. Practical skills assessments, simulations, and scenario-based exercises allow for a more comprehensive evaluation of trainees' abilities. These methods can reveal strengths and weaknesses that written exams might miss, providing instructors with valuable insights to inform future instruction and enhance the learning process. For example, observed practical demonstrations in handling different fire hoses under varying pressures in realistic fireground conditions allows for a more in-depth assessment of individual skills. Similarly, a simulation where recruits have to manage a multi-casualty incident with limited resources tests decision-making abilities, resource management, and teamwork.

Feedback mechanisms are also critical to the learning process. Constructive criticism should be delivered regularly, focusing on both individual and team performance. Regular feedback helps recruits understand their strengths and weaknesses, allowing them to target areas requiring improvement. The feedback mechanisms should be timely and action-oriented, not simply a summative assessment at the end of the training course. Moreover, it's important for the feedback to be delivered constructively and in a way that promotes growth and learning rather than creating negativity or discouragement. Constructive criticism from peers, self-reflection, and regular instructor check-ins can be included as well.

Finally, the curriculum should strive to instill a sense of purpose and professionalism. It's not enough to simply teach skills; the curriculum should also foster a commitment to lifelong learning and professional development. This can be achieved by integrating discussions of ethical considerations, leadership principles, and community engagement. Highlighting the importance of teamwork, communication and decision-making within the curriculum enhances professionalism and cultivates respect for the profession. By focusing on the human side of firefighting, the curriculum can inspire a deeper sense of commitment to the profession, reinforcing the recruits' dedication to serving their community.

The creation of a dynamic and engaging curriculum is an iterative process. Regular evaluation and revision are essential to ensure that the curriculum remains relevant and effective. Gathering feedback from instructors and recruits allows for continuous improvement and adaptation to evolving needs. Data analytics on student performance, identifying areas where understanding is strong or weak, can reveal the effectiveness of specific learning methods, allowing for the refinement of the curriculum design and improvement in the delivery of training. This iterative process ensures that the curriculum remains a living document, continuously adapting to the changing needs of the fire service and the evolving learning styles of its recruits. This process of continuous evaluation and refinement ensures the curriculum remains current, relevant, and effective. The result will be a training program that not only prepares highly skilled and competent firefighters but also cultivates a deep passion for the profession—a crucial investment in the future of the fire service.

Integrating the 'Why Before the How' philosophy into existing curricula requires a strategic and phased approach. It's not about a complete overhaul, but a thoughtful integration that leverages existing strengths while addressing areas needing improvement. The key is to focus on gradual change, ensuring buy-in from instructors and trainees alike. Beginning with pilot programs in specific modules allows for controlled implementation, data gathering, and iterative refinement. Successful pilots can then serve as models for wider adoption across the entire curriculum.

One effective starting point is to analyze existing training modules. Identify areas where the "why" is currently lacking or inadequately addressed. This might involve reviewing lesson plans, instructor notes, and student feedback. For example, a module on ladder safety might focus solely on the mechanics of raising and securing ladders. However, integrating the "why" could involve a discussion of potential rescue scenarios requiring ladder use, emphasizing the critical role ladders play in saving lives and mitigating risk. This context provides recruits with a deeper understanding and appreciation for the importance of ladder safety procedures.

Once these areas are identified, the next step involves re-designing the chosen modules. This involves reframing the learning objectives to prioritize the underlying rationale. Instead of simply teaching a skill, the objective should be to explain the underlying principles and its relevance to overall fire service operations. For instance, a module on hose handling might begin with a discussion of water pressure dynamics, the physics of water flow, and the relationship between hose handling techniques and effective fire suppression. This foundational knowledge then supports the instruction on specific techniques, enhancing understanding and retention. The redesigned module would then incorporate various learning methods to support the "why before how" approach.

Interactive simulations and scenario-based training exercises can be incredibly effective in illustrating the practical application of the "why." Consider the example of ventilation techniques. Instead of just explaining the mechanics of positive-pressure ventilation, a scenario could be created where recruits encounter a smoke-filled room, emphasizing the need for proper ventilation to ensure a safe entry for search and rescue teams. The scenario could involve multiple challenges, requiring them to choose the best ventilation technique based on the specific conditions. By directly linking the theoretical understanding of ventilation techniques to the practical consequences of effective and ineffective ventilation, the importance of the "why" becomes immediately apparent.

The incorporation of real-world case studies and examples is another powerful tool. Analyzing past incidents, where poor understanding of fundamental principles led to negative outcomes, can underscore the importance of mastering the "why." For example, a case study focusing on a fire where improper ventilation led to flashover, resulting in injuries to firefighters, can highlight the importance of understanding ventilation dynamics and the consequences of improper technique. Alternatively, case studies demonstrating effective use of specific skills or the importance of teamwork can inspire and motivate.

The integration of technology plays a significant role in delivering this updated approach. Augmented reality (AR) apps can overlay contextual information onto real-world equipment or scenarios. For example, an AR app could display the water pressure dynamics within a fire hose during a training exercise, providing recruits with a visual representation of the concepts being taught. Virtual reality (VR) simulations can replicate high-risk situations, allowing trainees to experience the consequences of their decisions in a safe and controlled environment without jeopardizing their safety or the safety of others. These technologies can significantly enhance learning through active participation and immediate feedback. Furthermore, integration of online learning platforms allows for the delivery of interactive modules, quizzes, and collaborative learning exercises which reinforce the understanding of "why" and its application.

However, the successful integration of technology requires careful consideration. The technology needs to support, not replace, effective teaching. Training officers require proper training and support to use these technologies effectively. Furthermore, the chosen technology must be compatible with existing systems and accessible to all trainees.

This should include accessibility features for all types of learners and learning styles.

Assessing learning in this revised approach also requires a broader perspective. Moving beyond traditional written exams, formative assessments should be built into each module. These may include practical demonstrations, scenario-based evaluations, and peer feedback sessions. By using a variety of assessment methods, instructors can obtain a more holistic picture of trainees' understanding and skill acquisition. This could include scenarios where recruits have to evaluate a scene and determine the appropriate course of action based on their understanding of fundamental firefighting principles. This approach enables a more realistic evaluation of their comprehension and skill in applying the principles taught.

Constructive feedback is paramount throughout the learning process. Regular feedback loops, both from instructors and peers, should be incorporated. This feedback should be specific, action-oriented, and focus on both the "why" and the "how." For instance, if a recruit demonstrates an inadequate understanding of water pressure dynamics, feedback might focus on areas where their understanding is lacking and link this to the broader context of effective fire suppression. This approach fosters a growth mindset and encourages continuous improvement.

Finally, ongoing evaluation and refinement are crucial. Data collected from pilot programs, student feedback, and instructor observations should inform revisions to the curriculum. This iterative process ensures that the curriculum remains relevant, effective, and adapts to the evolving needs of both the fire service and the learners themselves. This cyclical process ensures continuous improvement and adaptation to new technologies and changing training needs. By tracking key performance indicators (KPIs), such as test scores, practical skills assessments, and overall student satisfaction, the effectiveness of the training can be measured accurately.

This phased, integrated approach ensures that the "Why Before the How" philosophy isn't simply an add-on but a fundamental shift in the way fire service training is delivered. It fosters a deeper understanding, increased engagement, and ultimately, a more competent and confident generation of firefighters. The result will not only be better trained firefighters but also a renewed passion for the profession – a vital investment in the future of public safety. The long-term goal is to build a training culture where recruits understand not only *how* to perform a task, but *why* it is crucial to their safety and the safety of the community they serve. This is not simply about improving skills; it's about fostering a deeper professional commitment and a lifelong pursuit of excellence. This approach goes beyond technical skills, promoting a commitment to continuous learning, ethical decision-making, and the importance of teamwork, leadership, and community engagement. This holistic approach prepares not just firefighters but leaders in their community. A well-structured and engaging curriculum designed with these principles in mind represents a significant investment in the safety and well-being of both the recruits and the communities they serve, ensuring the future of fire service remains robust and effective.

Developing well-defined learning objectives is paramount to effective curriculum design. These objectives should not simply state what recruits will *do* at the end of a training module, but rather what they will *know, understand, and be able to apply*. This requires a shift from a purely skills-based approach to one that integrates cognitive and affective learning domains. For instance, instead of an objective like "The recruit will be able to correctly connect a firehose to a hydrant," a more comprehensive objective might read: "The recruit will understand the principles of water pressure and flow dynamics, explaining their impact on fire suppression techniques, and will be able to correctly and safely connect a firehose to a hydrant under varying pressure conditions." The improved objective emphasizes understanding *why* certain procedures are followed, adding depth and context to the practical skill.

This approach aligns perfectly with the "Why Before the How" philosophy. By focusing on the underlying principles and their practical implications, we cultivate a deeper, more meaningful understanding that leads to improved retention and skill mastery. To achieve this, learning objectives should be SMART: Specific, Measurable, Achievable, Relevant, and Time-bound. For example, a specific objective should avoid vague terms and clearly articulate the expected outcome. A measurable objective allows for quantifiable assessment, such as "The recruit will correctly identify the appropriate ventilation technique in 8 out of 10 simulated scenarios." An achievable objective is realistic and attainable within the given timeframe and resources. Relevant objectives directly contribute to the overall learning outcomes and the specific needs of the fire service. Finally, time-bound objectives ensure the learning process has a clearly defined endpoint.

Once learning objectives are clearly defined, we must develop corresponding assessment criteria. These criteria define how we will measure the achievement of the objectives. They shouldn't simply focus on whether a recruit can perform a task but should assess their understanding of the underlying principles. A variety of assessment methods should be employed to provide a comprehensive evaluation. These could include:

Written Examinations: These can assess theoretical understanding of concepts and principles. However, these should be designed to test understanding beyond simple memorization, requiring application of knowledge to novel scenarios. Instead of asking for definitions, questions should probe understanding of application and the consequences of choosing alternative strategies. For example, instead of asking "Define positive pressure ventilation," a question could ask: "Describe a scenario where positive pressure ventilation would be the most appropriate technique and explain why other methods would be less effective."

Practical Demonstrations: These allow for the assessment of practical skills and their application in realistic scenarios. The assessment rubric should clearly outline the expected performance levels, differentiating between competent, proficient, and expert levels of skill. For example, the assessment of a hose handling demonstration would assess not only the correct technique, but also the speed, efficiency and safety of the operation, all of which would be judged on a numerical scale. Further, the assessor should ask questions designed to test the theoretical understanding underpinning the procedure being demonstrated.

Scenario-Based Evaluations: This immersive approach simulates real-world fireground situations, allowing recruits to demonstrate their ability to apply knowledge and skills in a dynamic environment. The scenarios should be designed to assess decision-making skills, problem-solving abilities, and teamwork. The assessment rubric would consider factors like scene size-up, risk assessment, decision making, and the effective use of resources. These scenarios should involve a debrief session in which recruits are questioned and reflect on their decision-making process and why they chose the approach they did.

Peer and Self-Assessments: These methods promote reflective learning and offer valuable insights into a recruit's self-awareness and ability to receive and process feedback. Peer assessment allows for collaborative learning and promotes critical evaluation skills. These could involve recruits working in small groups to analyze each others performance in specific tasks, providing detailed feedback based on the assessment criteria. Self-assessment encourages self-reflection and helps recruits identify areas where they excel and where they need improvement.

Portfolio Assessments: This involves collecting evidence of a recruit's learning over time, including written work, practical demonstrations, and reflections on learning experiences. This allows for a holistic assessment and provides a more detailed understanding of the recruit's progress. This will give a more accurate picture of the recruits learning journey and how their understanding has developed over time.

The assessment criteria should be clearly communicated to the recruits from the outset, ensuring transparency and setting clear expectations. Rubrics and checklists can be used to make the assessment process more objective and consistent. Feedback should be provided promptly and constructively, focusing not only on areas for improvement, but also on strengths and successes. This feedback should be specific, action-oriented, and relate directly back to the learning objectives and the underlying principles.

Furthermore, the assessment process should be integrated throughout the training program, not just reserved for the end. Formative assessments, conducted during the learning process, allow for timely feedback and adjustments to teaching strategies.

Summative assessments, typically conducted at the end of a module or training program, provide a comprehensive evaluation of learning outcomes. A balanced approach using both formative and summative assessments offers a more accurate and comprehensive picture of a recruit's learning progress.

The assessment methods should be carefully selected to align with the learning objectives and the specific skills being assessed. For example, a module on hazardous materials would require a different assessment approach compared to a module on basic firefighting techniques. The assessment process itself should be designed to reflect the values and principles of the fire service, promoting integrity, professionalism, and teamwork. For instance, peer assessments must be undertaken with sensitivity and constructive feedback, reflecting a collaborative and supportive learning environment.

In conclusion, developing clear and measurable learning objectives and corresponding assessment criteria is crucial to the success of any fire service training program. By integrating the "Why Before the How" philosophy, we move beyond a purely skills-based approach to a more holistic model that emphasizes understanding, application, and critical thinking. Utilizing a variety of assessment methods and providing timely and constructive feedback ensures recruits gain a deep and lasting understanding of firefighting principles, preparing them to become competent, confident, and capable firefighters committed to the safety and well-being of their communities. This integrated approach helps to establish a culture of continuous learning and improvement, which is essential for maintaining high standards of professional excellence within the fire service. The long-term investment in this comprehensive training approach will lead to safer and more effective firefighting operations.

Creating adaptable and modular training programs is crucial in today's dynamic fire service environment. The rigidity of traditional, monolithic training curricula often fails to accommodate the diverse learning styles of recruits and the ever-evolving demands of the profession. A modular approach offers unparalleled flexibility, allowing for customization to specific departmental needs, individual learning paces, and even unforeseen circumstances such as equipment shortages or changes in operational priorities. This flexibility also extends to integrating new technologies and incorporating evolving best practices in fire safety and emergency response.

The foundation of a modular system lies in breaking down the overall curriculum into smaller, self-contained modules. Each module focuses on a specific learning objective, complete with its own set of learning activities, assessments, and resources. For example, instead of a single, week-long course on ventilation, the curriculum might include separate modules on:

Fundamentals of Ventilation: This module would cover the theoretical principles of ventilation, different ventilation techniques, and the physics of smoke and heat movement. Assessment would involve written examinations testing understanding of these concepts and their application in varied scenarios.

Positive Pressure Ventilation (PPV): This module would focus specifically on PPV techniques, including equipment setup, operation, and safety procedures. Assessment would include practical demonstrations, focusing on safe and efficient execution of the techniques, along with scenario-based evaluations to test decision-making in real-world situations.

Negative Pressure Ventilation (NPV): This would parallel the PPV module, but concentrate on NPV techniques, again with a mix of practical demonstrations and scenario-based assessments.

Hydraulic Ventilation: This module would cover the principles and techniques of hydraulic ventilation, its applications and limitations, and safety considerations. Assessment would be similar to the other ventilation modules, including written and practical components.

Ventilation Safety and Risk Management: This module would address the inherent risks associated with ventilation, emphasizing safety protocols, risk assessment, and crew coordination. Assessment would likely involve scenario-based evaluations and discussions concerning risk mitigation strategies.

This modular structure allows for greater flexibility in sequencing. Instructors can adjust the order of modules to suit specific needs, prioritizing certain areas based on departmental priorities or the specific strengths and weaknesses of the recruits. Some recruits might benefit from revisiting fundamental modules before progressing, while others might excel and quickly move through the foundational material. This personalized approach respects individual learning styles and optimizes the learning experience for each recruit.

The modular design also enhances the program's resilience to unexpected disruptions. If equipment malfunctions or a training facility becomes unavailable, instructors can easily substitute or reschedule modules without compromising the entire training program. This flexibility is invaluable in addressing unforeseen circumstances, minimizing delays and maintaining training momentum.

Furthermore, the modularity facilitates the easy integration of new technologies and updated procedures. New training materials, software simulations, or virtual reality exercises can be added or substituted within individual modules without requiring a complete overhaul of the entire curriculum. This ensures the training program remains current and relevant to the latest advancements in firefighting techniques and safety regulations.

The development of effective modules requires careful consideration of several factors. Clear and concise learning objectives must be defined for each module, ensuring they align with the overall curriculum goals. Learning activities should be diverse and engaging, incorporating a mix of lectures, demonstrations, simulations, and hands-on practice. Assessment methods should be varied to accurately measure the achievement of learning objectives, including written examinations, practical demonstrations, scenario-based exercises, and peer assessments.

Finally, a robust system for tracking and managing progress is essential. This might involve the use of a learning management system (LMS) to track individual recruit progress through each module, provide feedback, and facilitate communication between instructors and recruits. Regular evaluations of the modules themselves are crucial to ensure they remain effective and relevant, adapting as needed based on feedback from instructors, recruits, and performance data.

The benefits of modular, flexible training programs extend beyond the immediate training environment. The enhanced adaptability allows fire departments to better respond to evolving community needs, such as changes in building construction, population density, or the emergence of new hazards. The personalized learning approach helps to cultivate more confident and competent firefighters, better equipped to handle the complexities and challenges of modern emergency response. The ease of updating modules ensures the department maintains a high level of preparedness and is always at the forefront of fire safety best practices. Investing in this type of robust and adaptable training system ultimately translates to a more effective and safer fire service, better able to protect the communities they serve. This commitment to innovative and responsive training underscores the dedication to continuous improvement within the department, ensuring the highest standards of professionalism and operational excellence are upheld, ultimately benefiting the firefighters and the public they protect. The flexibility inherent in modular design promotes a dynamic and responsive training environment, ensuring that fire service training remains at the cutting edge of safety and proficiency. This in turn fosters a culture of continuous learning and self-improvement within the ranks, ultimately leading to a more capable, skilled, and confident firefighting force ready to meet any challenge.

Ensuring that our training programs not only meet but exceed nationally recognized fire service standards is paramount. This isn't simply a matter of compliance; it's about ensuring the safety and effectiveness of our firefighters and, ultimately, the communities we serve. National standards represent the culmination of years of research, experience, and best practices within the fire service, providing a benchmark for excellence that we must consistently strive to achieve. These standards cover a wide range of areas, from initial recruit training to ongoing professional development, encompassing everything from hazardous materials handling to advanced rescue techniques. Our curriculum must reflect this breadth and depth, ensuring that our recruits receive the comprehensive training necessary to operate safely and effectively in a multitude of emergency scenarios.

Aligning with these standards requires a multi-faceted approach. Firstly, it demands a thorough and ongoing review of the national standards themselves. These standards are not static documents; they evolve and are updated to reflect advancements in technology, changes in building construction, and emerging hazards. Our training programs must remain dynamic and responsive to these changes, ensuring that we are continuously updating our curriculum to remain current and relevant. This requires active participation in professional development opportunities for training officers, allowing them to stay abreast of the latest changes and best practices. Regular attendance at conferences, workshops, and training seminars is essential to maintaining this crucial awareness.

Furthermore, a dedicated process for curriculum review and revision is vital. This process should involve input from multiple stakeholders, including instructors, firefighters with field experience, and representatives from relevant national organizations. This collaborative approach ensures that the curriculum not only meets national standards but also incorporates practical considerations and real-world perspectives. Regular audits and evaluations of our training programs, benchmarked against national standards, are critical for identifying areas of strength and areas needing improvement. These evaluations should be data-driven, utilizing metrics such as recruit performance on assessments, incident response data, and feedback from instructors and graduates to inform adjustments and improvements.

The integration of technology plays a critical role in ensuring compliance and enhancing training effectiveness. The use of sophisticated simulation software, virtual reality training environments, and online learning platforms allows us to create realistic and engaging training experiences. These technologies offer opportunities to replicate high-risk scenarios in a safe environment, allowing recruits to develop critical decision-making skills and improve their proficiency without compromising their safety. Moreover, technology facilitates the efficient dissemination of updates to the curriculum, ensuring that everyone involved has access to the most current information.

One crucial aspect of aligning with national standards involves the assessment of recruit competency. The assessment methods we employ must accurately reflect the skills and knowledge outlined in these standards. This goes beyond simple written examinations; it requires the implementation of practical evaluations that assess recruits' abilities in a realistic context. Scenario-based training exercises, realistic emergency simulations, and peer evaluations are all valuable tools that provide comprehensive assessments of recruit competency. The rigorous nature of these assessments ensures that graduates are truly prepared to meet the challenges of the profession.

Beyond the initial recruit training, aligning with national standards extends to ongoing professional development. Firefighters must receive continuous training throughout their careers to maintain their skills and knowledge. This necessitates the establishment of a robust continuing education program that provides opportunities for professional development, skill enhancement, and specialization. This ongoing training is crucial for keeping our firefighters abreast of the latest techniques, technologies, and safety procedures, ensuring that they are always prepared to face evolving challenges. Regular refresher courses, specialized training in specific areas, and opportunities for advanced certification are all key components of a successful continuing education program.

A crucial element often overlooked is the documentation of our training programs. Comprehensive documentation is essential not only for meeting national standards but also for demonstrating accountability and transparency. This documentation should include a detailed curriculum outlining learning objectives, training methods, and assessment strategies. It should also include records of recruit participation, performance data, and feedback from instructors and graduates. This detailed documentation provides a clear and auditable trail of our training activities, demonstrating our commitment to excellence and ensuring that we maintain a high standard of training across all areas. Such meticulous records can also prove invaluable should any incidents occur in the field.

The financial investment in training is a significant commitment for any fire department. By aligning our training programs with national standards, we are maximizing the return on this investment. We are not only ensuring that our recruits are properly trained but also that we are minimizing risks and promoting safety. The long-term benefits of effective training far outweigh the initial costs, resulting in a more competent, confident, and safer firefighting force. The investment in training is an investment in the safety and well-being of our firefighters and the communities we serve. Therefore, alignment with national standards is not merely a procedural requirement; it is a strategic imperative.

Furthermore, the alignment with national standards fosters a culture of continuous improvement. By actively pursuing adherence to these standards, we are promoting a culture of excellence within our department. This culture encourages firefighters to constantly seek opportunities for professional development, to embrace innovation, and to strive for excellence in their work. This culture of excellence also enhances the overall morale and professionalism within the department, fostering a sense of pride and accomplishment among firefighters.

Finally, by demonstrating a commitment to national standards, we are enhancing the overall credibility and professionalism of our fire department. This commitment signals to the public that we are dedicated to providing the highest level of service, that we value the safety and well-being of our firefighters, and that we are actively working to improve our capabilities and effectiveness. This enhances the trust and confidence the community places in our department, reinforcing our critical role in protecting lives and property. In short, the alignment of our training programs with nationally recognized standards is not just a matter of compliance, it's a critical element in building a high-performing, safe, and trustworthy fire service.

Chapter 10: Leadership and Management in Fire Service Training

Effective leadership is the cornerstone of any successful fire service training program. It's not simply about assigning tasks and monitoring progress; it's about cultivating a culture of learning, fostering collaboration, and inspiring a passion for the profession. Effective leaders in this context are more than just instructors; they are mentors, motivators, and role models who guide recruits through the rigorous demands of fire service training, shaping them into competent and confident firefighters.

One of the key aspects of effective leadership is creating a positive and supportive learning environment. This involves fostering open communication, actively soliciting feedback from recruits, and addressing concerns promptly and fairly. A safe space where recruits feel comfortable asking questions, expressing their doubts, and sharing their experiences is essential for maximizing learning and minimizing anxieties. This environment requires a leader who is approachable, empathetic, and genuinely invested in the success of each individual recruit. It means creating an inclusive atmosphere that values diversity of thought and experience, recognizing that different learning styles and backgrounds contribute to a richer learning experience for everyone.

Furthermore, effective leaders in fire service training programs actively promote teamwork and collaboration. Firefighting is inherently a team sport, requiring seamless coordination and mutual trust amongst individuals to effectively respond to emergencies. Therefore, training must mirror this team dynamic, incorporating exercises that emphasize collaboration, communication, and problem-solving within a team context. Leaders achieve this by designing group projects, encouraging peer-to-peer learning, and fostering a sense of shared responsibility among recruits.

Beyond fostering a positive learning environment, effective leadership involves establishing clear learning objectives and expectations. Recruits need to understand the "why" behind the training, not just the "how." Leaders who explain the rationale behind specific techniques, connect theoretical concepts to practical applications, and highlight the real-world relevance of the training create a more engaged and motivated learning experience. This understanding fosters intrinsic motivation, driving recruits to actively participate in the learning process rather than simply completing assigned tasks. This approach aligns perfectly with the principles outlined in "Why Before the How," emphasizing the importance of understanding the underlying principles before mastering the technical skills.

Effective assessment and feedback are also integral components of effective leadership in fire service training. This extends beyond simple pass/fail grades. Constructive feedback should be delivered regularly and in a manner that supports learning and growth. Leaders should provide specific examples of both strengths and areas for improvement, offering guidance and resources to help recruits overcome challenges. They should create opportunities for self-assessment, enabling recruits to reflect on their performance and identify areas for development. This fosters self-awareness and promotes a continuous improvement mindset, critical for long-term success in the fire service.

In today's rapidly evolving technological landscape, fire service training programs must leverage the latest advancements to enhance learning effectiveness. Effective leaders understand this and are proactive in integrating technology into their training methodologies. This might involve incorporating interactive simulations, virtual reality exercises, online learning platforms, or data-driven assessment tools. Leaders who embrace technology demonstrate their commitment to continuous improvement and provide recruits with the skills and knowledge to operate in a technologically advanced world.

Another critical aspect of effective leadership is the ability to adapt to changing circumstances. The fire service, like any other profession, constantly evolves, with new technologies, techniques, and challenges constantly emerging. Leaders must be flexible and adaptable, modifying their training programs as needed to meet these evolving demands. This involves staying abreast of industry best practices, attending relevant conferences and workshops, and engaging with experts in the field. Adaptability also means responding effectively to unexpected events, such as equipment malfunctions or unforeseen logistical challenges, ensuring that training continues without significant disruptions.

The leadership role extends beyond the classroom or training facility. Effective leaders build strong relationships with other departments and organizations, fostering collaboration and partnerships that benefit the training program. This includes collaborating with local businesses, hospitals, or other emergency services to create realistic training scenarios and provide recruits with a comprehensive understanding of the multifaceted nature of emergency response. These relationships also open up opportunities for networking and knowledge sharing, enriching the learning experience for recruits.

Furthermore, effective leaders are adept at managing resources effectively. This includes personnel, equipment, and budgetary constraints. They develop a clear training plan that prioritizes essential skills and knowledge, optimizes the use of resources, and ensures that all training activities align with the overall departmental goals. Careful resource management ensures that the training program remains efficient, cost-effective, and sustainable.

Mentorship is another vital function of effective leadership in fire service training. Leaders should not only impart knowledge and skills but also serve as role models and mentors, guiding recruits through the challenges of the profession. This involves providing support, guidance, and encouragement, fostering a sense of camaraderie and belonging within the training program. Mentorship helps recruits to navigate the transition from recruit to firefighter, promoting their professional and personal growth.

Finally, leaders in fire service training programs must maintain high ethical standards and uphold the integrity of the profession. This involves demonstrating honesty, fairness, and respect in all interactions, upholding the values of the fire service, and promoting a culture of integrity within the training program. This sets the example for recruits and ensures that future firefighters adhere to the highest standards of ethical conduct.

In conclusion, effective leadership in fire service training is multifaceted, requiring a combination of pedagogical expertise, interpersonal skills, and a commitment to excellence. By fostering a positive learning environment, promoting collaboration, providing clear expectations, utilizing technology effectively, and demonstrating ethical conduct, leaders can create a training program that not only meets but exceeds expectations, preparing recruits to become confident, competent, and highly skilled firefighters. This leadership, in turn, ensures the safety and well-being of the community served. The success of any fire service hinges on the quality of its training, and the quality of its training hinges on the quality of its leadership. Investing in effective leadership is not just an investment in the training program; it's an investment in the future of the fire service and the communities it protects.

Motivating and supporting training staff is paramount to the success of any fire service training program. A highly motivated and well-supported training team translates directly into higher quality instruction, improved recruit engagement, and ultimately, safer and more effective firefighters. This requires a multifaceted approach that addresses both the individual needs of instructors and the overall functioning of the training department.

One of the most fundamental aspects of staff motivation is recognizing and rewarding their contributions. This goes beyond simple salary increases; it involves acknowledging their hard work, dedication, and the positive impact they have on the lives of recruits and the community. Regular verbal praise, written commendations, and opportunities for professional development can significantly boost morale and foster a sense of value. Publicly acknowledging outstanding achievements, such as exceptional teaching performance or the development of innovative training methods, can inspire other instructors and further cultivate a positive and supportive team environment. These recognitions should be specific and sincere, highlighting the individual's unique contributions and the positive impact they have had on the program. For example, if an instructor developed a particularly effective new training module that resulted in improved recruit performance on a critical skill, this achievement should be publicly recognized and lauded.

Furthermore, providing opportunities for professional growth is vital in maintaining a motivated and engaged training staff. This could involve sponsoring instructors to attend relevant conferences, workshops, or advanced training courses. This not only keeps their skills current but also demonstrates a commitment to their professional development. Providing access to updated resources, such as new textbooks, training manuals, and online learning platforms, ensures instructors can remain at the forefront of their field and incorporate the latest advancements into their teaching methods. Financial support for attending professional development activities, as well as providing the time for instructors to attend these events, are critical components in demonstrating a commitment to staff development. Consider establishing a mentorship program within the training department, pairing experienced instructors with newer staff to facilitate knowledge transfer, share best practices, and foster a strong sense of community.

Beyond professional development, fostering a collaborative and supportive work environment is crucial for staff morale. Regular team meetings, informal gatherings, and social events can help build camaraderie and a sense of belonging. Creating a space where instructors feel comfortable sharing ideas, concerns, and experiences is critical. This fosters open communication and ensures that challenges are addressed promptly and effectively. Implementing regular feedback mechanisms, such as anonymous surveys or formal performance reviews, can help identify areas for improvement and address any underlying issues that may be affecting staff morale. This feedback should be used constructively, focusing on identifying solutions and providing support rather than assigning blame. A strong team dynamic is invaluable in a high-pressure environment, and fostering this through teamwork and open communication provides a foundation for long-term success and job satisfaction.

Another essential element in supporting training staff is providing them with the necessary resources to do their job effectively. This includes ensuring they have access to the latest equipment, technology, and training materials. A well-equipped training facility, coupled with up-to-date training aids, significantly reduces instructors' workload and allows them to focus on delivering high-quality instruction. This also translates into a more engaging learning experience for recruits. For instance, investing in updated simulation technology allows instructors to create realistic training scenarios that mirror real-world emergencies, significantly enhancing the learning experience. This also ensures the training stays relevant and aligns with the current technological advancements within the fire service. Furthermore, providing adequate administrative support can free up instructors' time, allowing them to focus on teaching and student interaction, rather than getting bogged down in administrative tasks. A supportive administrative team can handle scheduling, logistics, material procurement, and other tasks, leaving instructors to concentrate on what they do best: training.

Addressing instructor workload is also critical. Overburdened instructors are less likely to be motivated and engaged. Implementing efficient scheduling practices, ensuring equitable distribution of responsibilities, and providing adequate breaks and time off are crucial for maintaining staff well-being. Regularly evaluating the workload and making necessary adjustments prevents burnout and maintains a positive and sustainable work environment. Implementing technology to streamline administrative tasks or utilizing peer teaching can distribute the workload more evenly, preventing one or two instructors from carrying a disproportionate burden. This demonstrates a commitment to the well-being of the training staff, valuing their contributions and recognizing the demanding nature of their roles. Understanding the needs of instructors and proactively addressing them is essential for fostering a positive and productive environment where staff feel valued and supported.

Open and honest communication is a cornerstone of supporting and motivating training staff. Regular meetings should provide opportunities for instructors to share their perspectives, express concerns, and contribute to decision-making processes. Active listening is essential, ensuring instructors feel heard and valued. This should be a two-way street; upper management should clearly communicate departmental goals, expectations, and changes to the training program. Transparency builds trust and strengthens the relationship between leadership and instructors. A clear and consistent communication strategy, encompassing regular updates, feedback sessions, and open forums for discussion, is vital for a well-functioning and highly motivated training team.

Beyond formal communication channels, cultivating a culture of mutual respect and appreciation is crucial. Creating a workplace environment that encourages collaboration, supports open dialogue, and celebrates both individual and team achievements is pivotal for maintaining a high level of morale and motivation. This necessitates a leadership style that is both supportive and empowering, enabling instructors to take ownership of their work and feel a genuine sense of involvement in the overall success of the training program. Creating a positive team dynamic through social events, informal gatherings, and opportunities for team building also improves morale and builds a stronger sense of camaraderie. A supportive environment where instructors feel comfortable sharing ideas, addressing concerns, and seeking help from colleagues fosters a positive and productive atmosphere.

In summary, motivating and supporting training staff demands a comprehensive strategy that integrates various approaches. Recognition and rewards, professional development opportunities, a collaborative work environment, adequate resources, manageable workloads, clear communication, and mutual respect are all crucial components. By prioritizing these elements, fire service training departments can cultivate a highly motivated and dedicated team of instructors, leading to a more effective and impactful training program, resulting in better-prepared, safer, and more confident firefighters. Investing in the well-being and professional development
of training staff is not just an investment in their individual careers; it is an investment in the future of the fire service.

Building a culture of continuous improvement within a fire service training program requires a multifaceted approach, going beyond simply implementing new techniques. It necessitates a fundamental shift in mindset, embracing a philosophy of ongoing evaluation, adaptation, and innovation. This starts at the top, with leadership actively championing the pursuit of excellence and providing the necessary resources and support.

One crucial element is the establishment of clear, measurable goals and objectives for the training program. These should align with the overall strategic goals of the fire department, encompassing key performance indicators (KPIs) that track the effectiveness of training initiatives. Examples of relevant KPIs could include recruit proficiency scores on practical skills assessments, successful completion rates of training modules, incident response times following training, and feedback from both instructors and trainees regarding training effectiveness. The regular monitoring and analysis of these KPIs provide valuable insights into areas of strength and weakness within the training program, identifying areas ripe for improvement. This data-driven approach ensures that improvements are targeted and impactful, maximizing the return on investment in training resources.

Regular program reviews are essential for maintaining momentum in continuous improvement. These reviews should involve not just training staff but also operational firefighters, who can provide valuable insights into the practical application of training in real-world scenarios. Feedback mechanisms should be diverse, encompassing formal performance reviews, anonymous surveys, focus groups, and informal discussions. These should specifically address the relevance, effectiveness, and efficiency of the training curriculum and its delivery methods. Analysis of the feedback should be systematic and objective, focusing on actionable insights rather than subjective opinions. For instance, if feedback consistently points to a particular training module being confusing or ineffective, this should trigger a thorough review and revision of the module, potentially incorporating new teaching methodologies or different learning materials.

The incorporation of innovative teaching methodologies is crucial for fostering a culture of continuous improvement. This involves actively exploring and adopting new training techniques, technologies, and learning resources. This might involve integrating virtual reality simulations to create realistic training scenarios, utilizing gamification techniques to enhance engagement and motivation, or adopting blended learning approaches that combine online learning with hands-on practical training. Regular professional development for instructors is essential in this process, providing them with opportunities to learn about new teaching methodologies and best practices. This could involve attending conferences, workshops, or online courses focusing on adult learning principles, instructional design, and the use of technology in training. The department should actively encourage instructors to explore and implement these new techniques, providing the resources and support needed for successful implementation.

Furthermore, fostering a culture of open communication and collaboration is paramount for continuous improvement. This requires creating an environment where instructors feel comfortable sharing their ideas, concerns, and experiences without fear of retribution. Regular team meetings, informal discussions, and collaborative projects can foster a sense of shared ownership and collective responsibility for the training program's success. Establishing a system for capturing and sharing best practices is essential. This could involve a dedicated online platform or a regular newsletter highlighting innovative training methods, successful teaching strategies, and lessons learned from past experiences. This ensures that effective techniques are disseminated throughout the department, avoiding redundant effort and maximizing the positive impact of successful training innovations.

Technology plays a significant role in enabling continuous improvement. Investing in a Learning Management System (LMS) can significantly streamline administrative tasks, track learner progress, and provide valuable data for assessing training effectiveness. Data analytics from the LMS can be used to identify individual student strengths and weaknesses, allowing for personalized learning experiences and targeted interventions. The data can also inform curriculum revisions, ensuring that training materials are relevant, engaging, and effective. Furthermore, the use of technology can enhance communication and collaboration among training staff, facilitating the sharing of best practices and ensuring that all instructors are using the most up-to-date teaching materials and methodologies.

Finally, continuous improvement is not a one-time endeavor but an ongoing process. It requires a commitment to ongoing evaluation, reflection, and adaptation. Regularly assessing the training program against established benchmarks, evaluating the impact of changes and innovations, and adapting to the ever-evolving needs of the fire service ensures that the training program remains relevant, effective, and prepares firefighters for the challenges they face. By embedding continuous improvement into the very fabric of the fire service training program, departments can ensure that they are consistently producing highly skilled, well-prepared, and confident firefighters ready to face the demands of their challenging profession. This commitment to excellence not only benefits the firefighters themselves but also enhances the safety and security of the communities they serve. The cycle of continuous improvement is not merely a process of refining current practices; it is a dynamic journey of ongoing innovation and adaptation, vital to maintaining a high standard of fire service training. By embracing this mindset, fire service training programs can achieve not just incremental improvements but transformational changes in firefighter readiness and performance.

Effective resource management is paramount to delivering high-quality fire service training. It's not simply about acquiring the latest equipment or technology; it's about strategically allocating resources to maximize their impact on training effectiveness and ultimately, firefighter safety and community protection. This requires a multifaceted approach encompassing careful planning, efficient procurement, proactive maintenance, and continuous evaluation.

Firstly, comprehensive planning is the bedrock of sound resource management. Before acquiring any resource, whether it's a new training simulator, specialized equipment, or software, a thorough needs assessment should be conducted. This assessment should identify the specific training needs of the department, the existing resources available, and any gaps that need to be filled. The assessment should involve input from all stakeholders, including instructors, firefighters, and even community members, to ensure a comprehensive understanding of the training requirements. This collaborative approach leads to more informed decisions and a greater likelihood of successful resource allocation.

Once the needs assessment is complete, the next step involves developing a detailed budget that aligns with the identified needs. This budget should prioritize essential resources that directly contribute to achieving training goals. It's crucial to distinguish between "wants" and "needs," focusing on resources that will have the greatest impact on training effectiveness. For example, investing in a high-fidelity burn building simulator might be a "want," while investing in updated personal protective equipment (PPE) is a clear "need." Prioritizing needs ensures that limited resources are used effectively.

Budgeting also requires careful consideration of both initial costs and ongoing maintenance expenses. Purchasing advanced training equipment may seem cost-effective initially, but ongoing maintenance and repair costs can significantly impact the overall budget. Therefore, it's vital to factor in these long-term costs when making purchasing decisions. Conducting thorough research on equipment reliability and maintenance requirements is crucial to avoid unforeseen financial burdens.

Efficient procurement is another critical aspect of resource management. This involves establishing clear procurement procedures that ensure transparency, accountability, and cost-effectiveness. Utilizing competitive bidding processes can help secure the best value for money when purchasing equipment or services. It is also important to ensure compliance with all relevant regulations and policies to avoid potential legal issues.

Beyond the initial acquisition, proactive maintenance is crucial for ensuring the longevity and effectiveness of training resources. This involves establishing a regular maintenance schedule for all equipment and facilities, including preventative maintenance to avoid costly repairs. This not only extends the life of equipment but also ensures that training can continue without disruption. A well-maintained training facility and equipment contribute significantly to a safer and more effective training environment.

In addition to physical resources, effective resource management also encompasses human resources. Investing in the professional development of instructors is crucial for maintaining high-quality training. This includes providing instructors with opportunities for continuing education, attending relevant conferences and workshops, and obtaining advanced certifications. This investment in instructors' skills and knowledge ensures that they can deliver the most up-to-date and effective training.

The efficient management of training materials is also a significant aspect of resource management. This includes organizing and storing materials effectively, ensuring they are readily accessible to instructors and trainees. Utilizing a digital learning management system (LMS) can streamline this process, allowing for easy access to course materials, updates, and tracking of trainee progress. A well-organized and easily accessible resource library is essential for facilitating smooth and efficient training operations.

Data-driven decision-making is vital in effective resource management. Tracking key performance indicators (KPIs) associated with training, such as trainee performance on assessments, completion rates, and feedback from trainees and instructors, helps to evaluate the effectiveness of resource allocation. Analyzing this data can identify areas where resources are being used effectively and areas where improvements are needed. This allows for informed decisions regarding resource allocation in future budget cycles.

Finally, continuous evaluation is crucial for adapting and improving resource management strategies. Regular reviews of the training program and its associated resource allocation can reveal areas needing adjustment. This may involve re-allocating resources to address emerging needs or improving training methods based on feedback and performance data. A flexible and adaptive approach to resource management ensures that the program remains relevant, efficient, and effective in meeting the evolving needs of the fire service.

Budget allocation for fire service training is a complex process that requires careful consideration of various factors. This includes identifying the necessary training resources, prioritizing training needs based on risk assessment and operational requirements, determining the cost-effectiveness of different training options, and projecting long-term costs of training programs.

It's crucial to engage in collaborative budgeting exercises involving stakeholders from all levels of the department, including trainers, firefighters, and administrative personnel. This will foster a better understanding of needs and priorities, resulting in a more comprehensive and effective budget.

Furthermore, the budget should reflect the department's overall strategic goals and priorities. For example, if the department is focused on improving response times, the budget should reflect this by allocating resources to training programs specifically designed to enhance speed and efficiency in emergency response. The budget should also reflect the department's commitment to innovation and technology adoption, by allocating funds for training in cutting-edge techniques and equipment.

Regular budget reviews are necessary to ensure that the training budget remains aligned with evolving departmental needs and priorities. This involves tracking expenditures against the approved budget, assessing the effectiveness of training programs, and making adjustments as needed. This cyclical review process ensures that the allocated resources are always optimized for maximum impact on training effectiveness. It also facilitates transparency and accountability within the budgeting process.

Moreover, exploring alternative funding sources, such as grants and external partnerships, can supplement departmental budgets. Seeking out grants for specialized training equipment or programs can significantly augment the department's training capabilities. Partnerships with local colleges or universities can provide access to specialized instructors and facilities, reducing the financial burden on the department. Strategic alliances with community organizations can also contribute to expanding training resources and improving community engagement.

Finally, creating a culture of fiscal responsibility within the fire service training program is essential for effective budget management. This involves encouraging instructors and trainees to make conscious choices regarding resource utilization, fostering a mindset of conservation and efficiency. It also involves implementing measures to minimize waste and maximize the lifespan of training equipment and materials. By promoting a culture of responsible resource management, departments can enhance the long-term sustainability of their training programs while optimizing their training budget.

Effective collaboration and communication are the lifeblood of any successful fire service training program. While resource management lays the foundation for a robust program, it is the synergy between team members that truly elevates training effectiveness and fosters a positive learning environment. This section delves into the critical role of communication and collaboration in creating a cohesive and high-performing training team.

Firstly, fostering open and honest communication is paramount. This goes beyond simply disseminating information; it involves creating an environment where every member feels comfortable expressing their ideas, concerns, and feedback without fear of judgment. This requires a conscious effort from leadership to actively listen to team members, value their perspectives, and create channels for open dialogue. Regular team meetings, informal brainstorming sessions, and dedicated feedback mechanisms are vital for ensuring a free flow of information. These interactions should not be limited to formal settings; fostering a culture of informal communication, where instructors and support staff feel comfortable approaching each other with questions or concerns, is equally crucial.

Moreover, effective communication should utilize a variety of methods to cater to different learning styles and preferences. While face-to-face communication remains vital for building rapport and fostering teamwork, incorporating digital communication tools can greatly enhance efficiency and accessibility. Utilizing platforms like email, instant messaging, and collaborative document-sharing tools can streamline communication, particularly when dealing with geographically dispersed teams or addressing time-sensitive matters. For example, using a shared online calendar for scheduling training sessions and coordinating logistics prevents scheduling conflicts and improves coordination across the team. Adopting a centralized communication system ensures that critical information, such as changes to training schedules or updates on equipment maintenance, is efficiently disseminated to all team members, minimizing potential disruptions to the training program.

Furthermore, the use of visual aids and multimedia in communication is invaluable.

Fire service training frequently involves complex procedures and technical concepts. Using visual aids such as diagrams, videos, and interactive simulations can significantly enhance comprehension and retention. For example, using a 3D model of a building to explain fire behavior and spread patterns can be significantly more effective than a simple lecture. Similarly, videos of real-life fire scenarios can demonstrate the application of techniques in a realistic context, enhancing engagement and understanding. Employing multimedia in training materials and internal communications ensures that everyone has access to engaging and easily digestible information.

Collaboration within the training team extends beyond simply communicating; it necessitates a shared understanding of goals, responsibilities, and roles. This requires establishing clear lines of authority and responsibility while simultaneously fostering a collaborative spirit. Defining specific roles and responsibilities within the training team ensures everyone understands their contribution and reduces the likelihood of overlap or neglect of tasks. For instance, one team member might focus on curriculum development, while another might specialize in equipment maintenance. Clearly defining these roles helps to streamline the workflow and ensure that each task is addressed efficiently.

Beyond individual roles, effective collaboration requires establishing shared goals and objectives. This necessitates a common understanding of the overall mission and the specific training outcomes that are to be achieved. Setting clear, measurable, achievable, relevant, and time-bound (SMART) goals provides a roadmap for the training team, focusing their efforts and improving accountability. Regular progress monitoring and feedback sessions help the team stay on track and address any emerging challenges collectively. For example, the team might set a goal to improve trainee performance on a specific skill by a certain percentage within a defined time frame. Tracking progress against this goal and adjusting the training methods as necessary allows for continual improvement.

Effective teamwork necessitates mutual respect and trust among team members. This requires creating a safe and inclusive environment where every member feels valued and respected. Encouraging open dialogue, valuing diverse perspectives, and actively addressing conflicts constructively fosters a supportive team environment. Regular team-building activities can strengthen relationships between team members, improving communication and collaboration. For example, undertaking a practical, collaborative task, such as assembling a training prop, can foster teamwork and communication in a less formal setting.

Furthermore, embracing diverse learning styles and incorporating them into training methodologies is crucial. Recognizing that individuals learn differently ensures the inclusivity and effectiveness of training. This means using a variety of teaching methods, including lectures, demonstrations, simulations, and hands-on activities to cater to the diverse learning preferences within the training team. For example, while some individuals might learn best through visual aids, others might prefer hands-on experiences. Incorporating a mix of learning styles within the training programs benefits both the trainees and the instructors, ensuring that everyone benefits from a dynamic and engaging training experience.

The training team also benefits from incorporating constructive feedback mechanisms. Regular feedback sessions, both formal and informal, allow team members to share ideas, evaluate progress, and identify areas for improvement. This can involve peer reviews, supervisor feedback, and trainee evaluations, providing valuable insights that can be used to refine training methods and enhance team performance. A culture of continuous improvement allows the training team to adapt and adjust their strategies based on actual feedback, ensuring that the training program remains relevant and effective.

Finally, continuous professional development is an essential component of effective teamwork in fire service training. Providing instructors and support staff with opportunities for ongoing professional development ensures that the team stays abreast of the latest techniques, technologies, and best practices in fire service training. This can involve attending conferences, workshops, participating in online courses, or engaging in peer-to-peer learning. A commitment to continuous improvement at both the individual and team levels ensures that the fire service training program remains at the forefront of excellence and innovation. By investing in the professional development of its team, the fire service department demonstrates its commitment to providing high-quality training and improving public safety. This investment translates to a more confident, skilled, and adaptable workforce, better equipped to handle the challenges of fire service operations. The ongoing professional development of the training team is not merely a cost; it is an investment in the future of firefighter safety and community protection.

Chapter 11: Safety Considerations in Fire Service Training

Comprehensive risk assessment is the cornerstone of safe and effective fire service training. It's not simply a box-ticking exercise; it's a proactive, ongoing process that integrates seamlessly into every aspect of the training program. Before any training activity commences, a thorough assessment must be undertaken, identifying potential hazards and vulnerabilities. This involves a multi-faceted approach, considering the environment, equipment, and the trainees themselves.

The environmental assessment should meticulously examine the training location. Is it adequately lit and ventilated? Are there any potential trip hazards, such as uneven ground or debris? Are there nearby structures that could pose a risk? For outdoor training, weather conditions must be carefully considered. High winds, extreme temperatures, or inclement weather can significantly increase the risk of accidents. For indoor training, the structural integrity of the building should be verified, checking for any potential structural weaknesses or hazards. The presence of asbestos, lead paint, or other hazardous materials must also be investigated and appropriate precautions taken.

Equipment assessment is equally crucial. All equipment used in training, from personal protective equipment (PPE) to training props, should be meticulously inspected for damage or defects. Regular maintenance schedules should be in place, ensuring that all equipment is in optimal working order. This includes not only functional checks but also ensuring the equipment is appropriately sized and suitable for the trainees' physical capabilities. For instance, self-contained breathing apparatus (SCBA) must be properly fitted and checked for leaks, ensuring the safety of trainees during breathing apparatus training exercises.

Similarly, training props, such as burning structures or vehicles, should be designed and managed in a way that minimizes the risk of uncontrolled fire spread or collapse.

The assessment must also factor in the trainees' capabilities and experience levels. Are they adequately trained to perform the specific tasks involved in the exercise? Do they possess the necessary physical fitness levels to handle the demands of the training? Consideration of trainees' individual medical conditions and limitations is paramount. Prior to any high-intensity training, health questionnaires and physical fitness assessments may be necessary. Adapting training exercises to account for diverse physical capabilities promotes inclusion and minimizes the risk of injury. For example, modifications to certain exercises might be necessary for trainees with physical limitations, ensuring that the training is accessible to all while still maintaining effectiveness.

Once potential hazards have been identified, the next stage involves developing mitigation strategies. This is where the 'why' before the 'how' philosophy really shines. It's not enough to simply list safety precautions; trainees need to understand the rationale behind these measures. Explaining the 'why' fosters a deeper understanding and greater engagement with safety protocols, leading to better compliance and safer practices.

Mitigation strategies should be multi-layered, incorporating both preventative and reactive measures. Preventative measures aim to eliminate hazards or reduce the likelihood of accidents occurring. This might involve removing trip hazards, providing adequate lighting, using appropriate PPE, and implementing detailed safety briefings before each exercise. The safety briefings shouldn't be a dry recitation of rules; instead, they should engage the trainees, explaining the potential consequences of unsafe practices and emphasizing the importance of adherence to safety protocols. Using real-life examples of accidents caused by negligence can be powerful in driving home this message.

Reactive measures are designed to manage incidents should they occur. This requires having appropriate emergency procedures in place, including well-defined communication protocols, access to emergency medical services, and clearly marked assembly points. Trainees should be thoroughly trained in these procedures, practicing emergency response drills regularly to ensure that they are proficient in reacting appropriately in a crisis. Having readily available emergency equipment, such as first-aid kits and fire extinguishers, is also critical. Regular maintenance and inspection of this equipment should be part of the overall risk management plan.

The risk assessment and mitigation strategies should be documented meticulously. This documentation serves as a valuable record, allowing for continuous improvement and accountability. Regular review and updates of the risk assessment are crucial, particularly after any incidents or near misses, allowing for adjustments to be made in training protocols. This iterative approach ensures that the training remains safe and effective.

Beyond the immediate training environment, the larger context of risk management within the fire service needs consideration. This includes factors such as adequate staffing levels, access to resources and support systems, and the overall organizational culture promoting safety. For example, an adequate number of instructors or support personnel should be available during training exercises, ensuring sufficient supervision and support for trainees. Moreover, effective communication channels between the training team and other departments, such as emergency medical services, are critical in facilitating rapid response to any incidents.

The culture of safety must permeate every aspect of the fire service, from training exercises to live incidents. This includes regular safety meetings and training, reinforcing safety protocols and fostering a climate of accountability. Encouraging trainees to report hazards or near misses without fear of retribution is crucial in identifying and addressing potential problems before they escalate into incidents. Leading by example, with instructors consistently demonstrating safe practices, is essential in establishing a strong safety culture within the training environment.

Furthermore, the principles of continuous improvement should be integrated into the risk management process. After each training exercise, a post-training review should take place. This review should analyze the effectiveness of the risk assessment and mitigation strategies, identifying any areas for improvement. Feedback from trainees and instructors should be actively solicited and incorporated into future training plans. This iterative approach, combining regular assessment, adaptation, and learning, ensures that safety remains a paramount concern in all aspects of fire service training.

Finally, embracing technological advancements in risk assessment and mitigation is also critical. Software applications and data analysis tools can assist in identifying patterns and trends in incidents, allowing for more effective preventative measures to be implemented. For example, tracking data on training-related injuries can reveal areas where improvements in safety protocols are needed. The use of virtual reality (VR) and augmented reality (AR) technologies offers a safe and cost-effective way to train personnel in hazardous scenarios, mitigating the risks associated with live exercises. By integrating these technological advancements into the risk assessment and mitigation strategies, the fire service can continually improve safety in training and reduce risks for all involved. The ultimate goal is not just to prevent accidents, but to foster a culture of safety, where hazard identification and risk mitigation are seamlessly integrated into every aspect of fire service training. This creates a learning environment where trainees develop not only critical skills but also a deep-seated respect for safety, preparing them for the challenging and sometimes hazardous realities of firefighting.

Emergency procedures and response protocols are not mere add-ons to fire service training; they are the lifeblood of a safe and effective program. They represent the reactive component of our comprehensive risk management strategy, complementing the preventative measures discussed earlier. Their effectiveness hinges on meticulous planning, thorough training, and consistent practice. The goal isn't simply to have protocols in place, but to instill in every trainee an ingrained understanding of their importance and the ability to execute them flawlessly under pressure. This requires a shift from rote memorization to a deep, experiential understanding. We accomplish this through scenario-based training, realistic simulations, and a robust system of feedback and continuous improvement.

The first step in building a robust emergency response system is to define clear roles and responsibilities. Every individual involved in a training exercise—instructors, trainees, medical personnel, and even observers—should have a designated role and understand their responsibilities in an emergency. This clarity eliminates confusion and ensures a coordinated response. For instance, designated safety officers should be responsible for monitoring the exercise, identifying potential hazards, and immediately communicating any concerns to the training director. A designated communications officer should manage all communication channels, ensuring rapid and effective information flow among all participants. Having a clearly defined chain of command enhances the efficiency and effectiveness of emergency response.

Furthermore, establishing effective communication protocols is crucial. This involves specifying the methods of communication—radios, cell phones, whistles—and the protocols for reporting emergencies. Standardized terminology should be used to avoid ambiguity and ensure clear communication across different teams. Regular communication drills should be incorporated into the training schedule to ensure that all participants are familiar with the protocols and can communicate effectively under stress. The use of simulated emergencies, such as a sudden flare-up of a training fire or a trainee suffering a simulated injury, allows for practice and refinement of communication strategies.

Access to emergency medical services (EMS) is paramount. Before any training exercise, arrangements must be made to ensure prompt access to EMS. This may involve establishing a direct communication link with a local ambulance service, identifying the nearest hospital, and designating a meeting point for paramedics. A detailed emergency action plan (EAP) should be developed, outlining the steps to be taken in case of an injury or other emergency. The EAP should include contact information for EMS, designated assembly points, and procedures for managing injured trainees. Regular reviews and updates of the EAP should be conducted to ensure it remains relevant and effective. This includes incorporating lessons learned from past incidents or near misses.

Beyond EMS, having readily available first aid equipment and trained personnel is essential. Well-stocked first-aid kits should be strategically positioned throughout the training area, and all instructors should possess a current first-aid certification. Trainees should also receive basic first-aid training as part of their overall curriculum. This not only prepares them to respond to injuries during training but also equips them with valuable skills for their future careers. Regular inspections of first-aid equipment ensure that supplies are replenished and equipment remains in optimal working order.

The creation of clear assembly points is another critical element of emergency procedures. These points should be easily identifiable and safe locations where trainees can gather in the event of an emergency. They should be marked clearly on maps and signage throughout the training area, and trainees should be thoroughly familiar with their location. The choice of assembly points should consider various factors such as proximity to exits, potential hazards, and accessibility for injured personnel. Regular drills should be conducted to ensure trainees can quickly and safely reach the designated assembly points in case of an evacuation.

Regular drills and simulations are the cornerstone of effective emergency response training. These drills should not be infrequent, perfunctory exercises; rather, they should be realistic, challenging simulations that push trainees to their limits. These drills should incorporate a variety of scenarios, mimicking the unpredictable nature of emergency situations. For example, a drill might simulate a sudden fire spread, requiring trainees to evacuate a burning structure while dealing with simulated injuries. Post-drill reviews and debriefings are crucial to analyze the effectiveness of the response, identify areas for improvement, and reinforce key learning points.

The "why" before the "how" philosophy is equally important in emergency response training. Trainees shouldn't just be told what to do; they need to understand the rationale behind the protocols. Explaining the potential consequences of non-compliance, using real-life examples of accidents caused by improper emergency response, can significantly increase engagement and improve retention. This approach fosters a deeper understanding and a greater sense of ownership, leading to better adherence to procedures during actual emergencies.

Technological advancements also play a vital role in enhancing emergency response. For example, the use of GPS tracking devices can aid in locating trainees during evacuation drills, improving the speed and efficiency of the response. Wearable technology can monitor trainee vital signs during strenuous training exercises, providing early warning of potential medical emergencies. Furthermore, incorporating virtual reality (VR) and augmented reality (AR) technologies can provide a safe and controlled environment for practicing emergency response procedures without the risks associated with live exercises.

Post-incident analysis is a crucial step in continuous improvement. Following any incident, no matter how minor, a thorough investigation should be conducted to determine the root causes and identify areas for improvement in procedures, training, or equipment. This process should involve all participants, including trainees and instructors. The results of the analysis should be used to update the emergency action plan and training materials. This systematic approach ensures that the emergency procedures are constantly refined and improved, enhancing the safety of all involved in fire service training.

Finally, fostering a culture of safety is essential for the effectiveness of any emergency response system. This involves creating a climate where trainees feel comfortable reporting hazards or near misses without fear of reprisal. Open communication and a proactive approach to safety are key to preventing incidents before they occur. Regular safety meetings and training sessions reinforce protocols and ensure that safety remains a top priority. This comprehensive approach, integrating preventative measures with thorough emergency procedures and a culture of safety, ensures the safety and effectiveness of fire service training, equipping our future firefighters with the knowledge and skills needed to thrive in this challenging and demanding profession. The ultimate aim is not just to survive emergencies, but to prevent them, and if they do occur, to respond decisively and effectively, ensuring the safety of all involved.

The foundation of any effective fire service training program rests upon a commitment to safety, and that commitment begins with Personal Protective Equipment (PPE) and safety gear. This isn't simply about complying with regulations; it's about fostering a culture where safety is paramount, ingrained in every aspect of training, from the initial briefing to the final debrief. The proper use, maintenance, and understanding of PPE aren't just elements of a training program; they're the cornerstone upon which success and safety are built.

Our trainees, future firefighters, are our most valuable asset. The investment a fire department makes in its personnel extends far beyond salary and benefits; it includes comprehensive training that equips them with the knowledge, skills, and—crucially—the protection they need to face the inherent dangers of their profession. Providing them with the correct PPE and instilling in them a respect for its proper use is not merely a matter of compliance; it is a moral imperative. It's about safeguarding their well-being, ensuring their continued service, and ultimately, saving lives.

Let's begin with the basics. Every trainee must be properly fitted with their PPE. This is not a one-size-fits-all proposition. A proper fitting ensures the gear functions as designed, providing the maximum protection intended. Ill-fitting equipment can restrict movement, impair visibility, compromise thermal protection, or even become a hazard itself during a training exercise. Our training program includes a dedicated session on proper PPE fitting, utilizing experienced personnel to guide trainees through the process and to address individual needs. We employ a standardized fitting checklist ensuring consistent application across all trainees. This checklist includes specific measurements and checks for proper fit and functionality of all components. It's about finding the sweet spot between comfort and protection—equipment that's both comfortable enough to wear for extended periods and protective enough to withstand the rigors of fire service work.

Beyond the initial fitting, regular inspections are non-negotiable. Before every training exercise, each trainee must conduct a thorough self-inspection of their PPE, checking for any signs of damage, wear, or malfunction. This includes examining the structural integrity of the turnout coat and pants, checking the functionality of zippers, closures, and protective layers, inspecting the helmet for cracks or damage, and verifying the proper functioning of the self-contained breathing apparatus (SCBA). These self-inspections are not just a formality; they're a critical safety check that empowers trainees to take ownership of their safety. Instructors also conduct random inspections to supplement trainee self-checks, adding another layer to the overall safety net. Any damaged or malfunctioning equipment is immediately removed from service and replaced, with meticulous records kept to ensure traceability and accountability.

Maintenance goes beyond simple inspections. We emphasize the importance of proper cleaning and storage of PPE. Soiled gear is not only unpleasant but also compromises its effectiveness and longevity. Following each training exercise, trainees are required to clean their gear according to established procedures, using approved cleaning agents. This isn't just about keeping the gear clean; it's about extending its lifespan and maintaining its protective capabilities. Improper cleaning can damage the protective layers of the gear, rendering it less effective in a real-world emergency. Regular washing, drying, and storage in designated areas according to manufacturer's instructions are emphasized, ensuring both the longevity and effectiveness of their PPE.

Our training program goes beyond the 'how' to the fundamental 'why'. We emphasize the science and engineering behind the design and functionality of each piece of PPE. Understanding the protective qualities of each layer, from the outer shell to the thermal barrier, reinforces the importance of wearing it correctly and maintaining its integrity. We explain the principles of heat transfer and the protective mechanisms of various fabrics. We illustrate the dangers of compromised thermal protection through case studies of near-miss incidents where inadequately maintained PPE led to serious injury. We demonstrate the limitations of the equipment, reinforcing that PPE is not a guarantee of invincibility but rather a crucial layer of protection that demands respect and diligent maintenance.

The SCBA deserves special attention. It's arguably the most critical piece of PPE a firefighter uses, providing the lifeline of breathable air in hazardous environments. Our training covers the thorough inspection of the SCBA, including checking the air cylinder pressure, ensuring the regulator functions correctly, inspecting the mask seal, and understanding the proper donning and doffing procedures. We stress the critical importance of regular SCBA fit testing, which ensures that the mask provides a proper seal, preventing the inhalation of toxic gases. Beyond the technical aspects, we instill in our trainees the importance of practicing with the SCBA regularly. The more comfortable they are with their SCBA, the better they can perform under pressure, which is paramount in any emergency situation. We conduct regular drills and simulations that incorporate SCBA usage in realistic scenarios, emphasizing the importance of maintaining a calm demeanor and executing the procedures correctly under stress.

Beyond the individual pieces of PPE, we cover a wider range of safety gear, including eye protection, gloves, hearing protection, and footwear. Each item serves a vital role in protecting the trainee from various hazards. Eye protection shields against flying debris, sparks, and intense heat. Gloves offer protection against cuts, burns, and chemical exposure. Hearing protection safeguards against the noise generated by equipment and emergencies. Proper footwear provides support and stability, preventing falls and injuries on uneven terrain. The training emphasizes the importance of using the appropriate gear for each activity, underscoring the fact that one type of glove might be suitable for handling a hose but completely inadequate for handling hazardous materials.

The maintenance and care of these auxiliary safety items are as crucial as the care of SCBA and turnout gear. Gloves need to be inspected for cuts or tears, goggles for scratches or cracks, and footwear for wear and tear. We establish clear procedures for the inspection, cleaning, and replacement of these items, integrating them into the daily routines of the trainees. These measures aren't just about prolonging the life of these items; it is about fostering a meticulous and cautious approach to safety that translates into real-world competence.

Furthermore, our training program incorporates regular safety briefings and discussions to reinforce the importance of PPE and safety gear. These aren't just lectures; they're interactive sessions that involve trainees in problem-solving and scenario-based discussions. We encourage trainees to ask questions, share concerns, and contribute their own perspectives on safety issues. This collaborative approach fosters a stronger sense of ownership and responsibility towards their own safety and the safety of their colleagues. It is about building a shared understanding and commitment to a culture of safety that goes beyond rote memorization of procedures.

We believe in using a multi-faceted approach. We incorporate real-life case studies, sharing examples of injuries and fatalities that resulted from neglecting PPE or improper gear usage. These case studies aren't meant to instill fear but to provide a stark reminder of the potential consequences of complacency. We also utilize visual aids, such as photos and videos, to demonstrate the proper way to use and maintain various pieces of equipment. This visual reinforcement enhances understanding and retention, complementing the hands-on practical sessions.

Moreover, our program incorporates ongoing assessment and feedback. We regularly observe trainees during training exercises, providing immediate feedback on their PPE use and adherence to safety protocols. This continuous feedback loop allows us to identify areas for improvement and reinforce positive behaviors. We encourage trainees to report any incidents, near misses, or concerns without fear of reprimand. This open communication fosters a safe and supportive environment where safety is a shared responsibility.

Finally, we extend the emphasis on PPE beyond the immediate training setting. We stress the importance of proper PPE use in future career scenarios, bridging the gap between training and real-world applications. We reinforce the idea that the procedures and habits learned during training are not only crucial for safety in a controlled training environment but are vital for survival and success as a firefighter. This continuity strengthens the sense of responsibility and commitment to safety, shaping the future firefighters into safety-conscious professionals. The ultimate goal is not just to teach trainees about PPE, but to foster a deep-seated respect for its importance, to create firefighters who instinctively prioritize safety in everything they do.

Simulating realistic scenarios is crucial for effective fire service training, but it must be done safely. The goal is to replicate the pressures and challenges of real-world firefighting without exposing trainees to undue risks. This requires a meticulous approach, a layered safety net, and a constant awareness of potential hazards. We prioritize a phased approach, gradually increasing the complexity and intensity of simulations as trainees gain experience and competency.

Our simulations begin with basic scenarios in controlled environments. This might involve a controlled burn in a designated burn building, allowing trainees to practice hose handling, nozzle operation, and teamwork in a relatively safe setting. The burn building is meticulously designed with multiple points of egress, ensuring rapid evacuation if needed. Fire suppression systems, including sprinklers and fire extinguishers, are readily available as backup measures. Before each exercise, a thorough risk assessment is conducted, identifying potential hazards and establishing contingency plans. Experienced instructors are positioned strategically to observe trainee performance and intervene if necessary.

Every aspect of these initial simulations is carefully controlled. The intensity and duration of the controlled burns are carefully monitored to prevent the fire from escalating beyond the designated parameters. The amount of smoke produced is carefully managed to ensure good visibility and prevent respiratory risks. The layout of the burn building, with its clearly marked escape routes and strategically placed safety equipment, reinforces safety awareness.

As trainees gain experience, we progressively introduce more complex simulations. These could involve multiple-story structures, simulated vehicle fires, or confined space rescues. In these scenarios, the level of realism increases, but so does the emphasis on safety protocols. We utilize a combination of props, simulations, and controlled environments to create realistic scenarios without compromising safety. For example, a vehicle fire simulation might involve a decommissioned vehicle and controlled fuel sources, allowing trainees to practice extinguishing techniques without the risk of uncontrolled explosions or fuel spills.

Technology plays a significant role in enhancing realism while maintaining safety. Virtual reality (VR) and augmented reality (AR) technologies are increasingly valuable tools in our training program. These technologies allow trainees to experience various fire scenarios in a safe, controlled environment, reacting to dynamic situations without the risks associated with live fires. VR simulations can be particularly useful for practicing high-risk procedures, such as confined space rescues or high-angle rope rescues, allowing trainees to develop crucial skills in a safe virtual setting before progressing to real-world applications.

For instance, our VR training module for confined space rescues replicates the disorientation, claustrophobia, and limited visibility that firefighters experience in actual confined spaces. Trainees navigate virtual environments, using virtual tools and equipment to complete rescue tasks, receiving immediate feedback on their performance. This allows them to repeatedly practice techniques and build muscle memory in a low-risk setting, improving both their skills and their confidence in handling high-risk scenarios. Similarly, our AR training module for high-angle rescues allows trainees to visualize the rescue operation overlaid onto a real-world environment, providing them with a more comprehensive understanding of the rescue scenario and its complexities.

Beyond VR and AR, we employ other technological advancements to enhance safety. For example, we utilize sophisticated smoke machines to generate realistic smoke conditions, allowing trainees to practice navigation and search techniques without the harmful effects of real smoke. These machines are equipped with safety features to control smoke density and prevent oxygen depletion. This controlled environment allows trainees to focus on tactical skills, such as searching for victims in zero-visibility conditions, without the health risks associated with exposure to real smoke.

The use of advanced simulation technologies is complemented by a robust safety briefings and debriefings system. Before each simulation, trainees receive a thorough briefing that outlines the objectives of the exercise, the potential hazards, and the safety procedures to be followed. This briefing incorporates detailed instructions, visual aids, and practical demonstrations to ensure clear understanding. Following the simulation, a comprehensive debriefing is conducted to analyze the trainee performance, identify areas for improvement, and reiterate safety protocols. This debriefing session is an opportunity for trainees to ask questions, share concerns, and receive feedback on their performance in a non-threatening environment. This iterative process of briefing, training, and debriefing is crucial for ensuring a balance between realistic training and unwavering safety.

Effective communication is paramount during simulations. We utilize clear and concise communication protocols to ensure efficient coordination among trainees and instructors. The use of radios and hand signals enhances communication in high-stress situations, mirroring real-world practices. We also emphasize the importance of clear and concise communication to ensure everyone understands their roles and responsibilities during the simulation. This clear communication structure is practiced repeatedly during various stages of the training program, making it second nature to the trainees in times of pressure.

Safety monitoring throughout the simulation is critical. Multiple instructors are present during each exercise, continuously observing trainee performance and intervening if necessary. They monitor vital signs, equipment functionality, and overall safety protocols, ensuring prompt intervention in case of any incident. Instructors utilize both visual observation and technological monitoring to maintain comprehensive situational awareness. This constant monitoring process ensures that the safety of the trainees is not compromised during intense and potentially hazardous training exercises.

Beyond the immediate safety measures during simulations, we incorporate robust emergency response plans. This includes designated escape routes, readily available emergency equipment, and a well-defined communication system. Emergency medical personnel are also on standby, ready to provide immediate medical assistance if needed. The implementation of this well-structured emergency response protocol is a proactive approach to ensure the safety of the trainees in case of unforeseen incidents.

Furthermore, post-simulation analysis is crucial. This includes reviewing video recordings of the simulations, examining the performance of the trainees, and identifying areas for improvement in both training techniques and safety procedures. This analysis allows us to continually refine our training methodology, enhancing its effectiveness while maintaining the highest standards of safety. This continuous improvement cycle ensures that our training program stays current with emerging technologies and best practices in the fire service.

Finally, we emphasize the importance of continuous learning and professional development. Our training officers receive ongoing professional development to ensure they stay abreast of the latest safety protocols and training methodologies. This ensures that our training program always meets or exceeds industry standards, ensuring that we are continually improving the safety and effectiveness of our fire service recruit training. The ultimate goal is not only to create skilled and competent firefighters but also to create firefighters who prioritize safety in every aspect of their profession, making safety an inherent part of their professional identity.

Post-incident analysis is not merely a bureaucratic exercise; it's a critical component of continuous improvement in fire service training, a cornerstone of ensuring trainee safety and developing highly skilled, adaptable firefighters. The process begins immediately following any training exercise, no matter how seemingly minor. A thorough review of events, even those without apparent injury or equipment damage, offers invaluable insights into potential weaknesses in our safety protocols or the effectiveness of our training methodologies.

Our approach involves a multi-faceted review process. First, a preliminary debrief occurs on-site, immediately after the event. This informal gathering of instructors and participating trainees allows for a quick assessment of what transpired, focusing on the immediate safety implications. This rapid debriefing provides an opportunity to capture first-hand accounts, impressions, and even emotional responses—crucial information often lost in the delay of a formal report. It's a time to identify any immediate concerns, address any lingering anxieties amongst trainees, and ensure no one requires medical attention beyond initial observations. This immediate feedback loop is essential for fostering a safety-conscious culture where voicing concerns is encouraged and acted upon swiftly.

Following the preliminary debrief, a more formal, in-depth analysis is conducted. This typically involves a detailed review of all available data: video recordings from multiple angles, instructor observation notes, trainee feedback forms, incident reports, and any relevant equipment logs. This comprehensive dataset allows for a multifaceted examination of the incident, moving beyond simple narratives to a rigorous examination of underlying causes and contributing factors. For instance, if a minor equipment malfunction occurred during a live-fire exercise, we don't just note the malfunction. Instead, we investigate the root cause – was there inadequate maintenance, a flaw in the equipment design, insufficient training on equipment operation, or a failure in pre-exercise checks?

This investigation is not solely about assigning blame. Instead, it's about identifying system vulnerabilities. Did communication protocols break down? Were safety procedures inadequately communicated or understood by trainees? Did the simulation itself present unforeseen challenges or unrealistic expectations? Were there environmental factors, such as unexpected wind conditions or changes in ambient temperature, that impacted safety? By employing a root-cause analysis approach, we move beyond surface-level observations to identify systematic issues that require attention.

Technology plays a significant role in this post-incident analysis. High-definition video recordings from strategically placed cameras provide an objective record of the events. This visual data allows us to slow down and analyze critical moments in detail, scrutinizing trainee actions, instructor responses, and overall situational awareness. Sophisticated video analysis software can further enhance this process, providing detailed metrics on movement, timing, and the interactions between individuals. Such data analysis goes far beyond simple observation; it quantifies performance, identifying patterns and trends that might otherwise go unnoticed.

The use of data analytics isn't limited to video analysis. We also track key performance indicators (KPIs) throughout the training program, including the number and nature of incidents, the types of injuries sustained, and the effectiveness of safety protocols in preventing accidents. This quantitative data, when analyzed alongside qualitative data from debriefings and feedback forms, paints a complete picture of our training program's safety performance, allowing for data-driven decisions about improvements. This approach ensures our training methods are consistently evaluated, adjusted, and refined to enhance safety and increase effectiveness.

Furthermore, the findings from post-incident analysis are not kept within a closed circle of instructors. We actively share our findings with trainees, making it a participatory process. This shared learning experience fosters a sense of ownership and collective responsibility for safety. The open sharing of lessons learned, both successes and failures, reinforces a culture of safety and continuous learning. Instead of viewing incidents as isolated occurrences, we integrate them into the learning curriculum. We might incorporate real-world examples of incidents, anonymized to protect individual privacy, into training scenarios, using them as case studies for discussion and analysis.

This approach is particularly effective in emphasizing the importance of proactive risk management. Trainees learn to anticipate potential hazards, not just react to them. By actively participating in the analysis of past incidents, they develop critical thinking skills and a deeper understanding of the importance of safety protocols. This engagement converts passive learning into active engagement, increasing retention and building a strong safety culture from the foundation of recruit training.

However, the post-incident analysis is not a standalone process. It's integrated into a larger framework of continuous improvement. After a detailed review, we develop corrective actions, documenting specific improvements to our training procedures, equipment maintenance schedules, or safety protocols. These actions are not just documented; they're implemented and rigorously monitored to ensure their effectiveness. We track the impact of these changes, measuring their contribution to improved safety and training outcomes. This continuous monitoring allows us to refine our approach iteratively, constantly seeking enhancements to the safety and efficiency of our training program.

The commitment to continuous improvement extends beyond training methodology. We regularly review and update our emergency response plans, ensuring they remain relevant and effective. This involves drills, simulations, and regular reviews of emergency procedures to ensure that everyone knows their role and responsibilities in an emergency. This also includes reviewing and updating our emergency equipment, ensuring it is well-maintained, properly stored, and readily accessible.

Finally, and critically, the continuous improvement process also includes the training of our instructors. Regular professional development keeps our instructors abreast of the latest safety standards, training techniques, and emergency response procedures. This investment in our instructors' professional development is paramount. They are the front line of safety, and their knowledge, skills, and commitment to continuous learning directly impact the safety and training outcomes of our recruits. This cyclical process of training, analysis, improvement, and further training reinforces the dedication to a culture of safety and ensures a consistently high standard for our fire service recruit training program. The ultimate goal is a generation of firefighters who not only possess exceptional skills but also exemplify an unwavering commitment to safety, making it an intrinsic part of their professional identity.

Chapter 12: The Future of Fire Service Training

The integration of technology into fire service training is no longer a futuristic concept; it's a rapidly evolving reality. We've already seen the benefits of high-definition video analysis in post-incident reviews, but the potential extends far beyond this. Artificial intelligence (AI) and machine learning (ML) are poised to revolutionize how we train, assess, and prepare our firefighters for the complexities of modern emergencies.

AI-powered simulations offer a significant leap forward in training realism. Traditional simulations, while valuable, often lack the dynamic unpredictability of real-world emergencies. AI can introduce this unpredictability, creating scenarios that adapt in real-time to trainee actions. Imagine a simulated structure fire where the fire's behavior responds to the firefighters' tactical decisions – the spread of flames altering based on water application strategies, or the collapse of structural elements reacting to the weight and impact of rescue operations. This level of dynamic interaction makes training far more engaging and effective, forcing trainees to think critically and adapt to unforeseen challenges. Furthermore, AI can populate these simulations with virtual victims exhibiting realistic symptoms and reactions, enhancing the realism of rescue scenarios.

Beyond dynamic simulations, AI offers powerful tools for assessment and feedback. Through the analysis of video footage from training exercises, AI can identify subtle errors in technique or decision-making that might escape human observation. For example, an AI system could analyze a firefighter's movements during a search and rescue operation, flagging deviations from established protocols, such as improper use of a thermal imager or unsafe entry techniques. This detailed analysis provides instructors with concrete data to support their feedback, leading to more targeted and effective training interventions. The quantitative nature of AI-generated feedback also mitigates any potential for subjective bias, ensuring a fair and consistent evaluation of trainees' performance.

Machine learning algorithms, a subset of AI, can further enhance training effectiveness. By analyzing vast datasets of training performance, incident reports, and even social media trends, ML can identify patterns and correlations that might indicate areas of weakness or potential hazards. For example, ML could analyze data from past incidents to identify common contributing factors to firefighter injuries, providing valuable insights for refining safety protocols and training procedures. Moreover, ML algorithms can personalize training plans, adapting the curriculum and difficulty level to suit the individual strengths and weaknesses of each trainee. This personalized approach maximizes learning efficiency, ensuring that each trainee receives the specific training they need to succeed.

The use of virtual reality (VR) and augmented reality (AR) technologies is also transforming fire service training. VR allows trainees to experience realistic scenarios in a safe and controlled environment, from navigating smoke-filled buildings to operating complex equipment under pressure. The immersive nature of VR enhances engagement and allows trainees to practice critical skills without the risks associated with live training exercises. Meanwhile, AR can overlay digital information onto the real world, providing firefighters with real-time data during training exercises or even actual emergencies. Imagine firefighters equipped with AR headsets that display thermal images, structural blueprints, and the location of other team members directly onto their field of view, enhancing situational awareness and improving coordination.

The integration of these emerging technologies doesn't just improve the quality of training; it also enhances the efficiency of the training process. AI-powered systems can automate administrative tasks, freeing up instructors to focus on providing personalized instruction and mentoring. Data analytics can provide real-time feedback on training effectiveness, allowing for prompt adjustments and improvements. These efficiency gains are crucial, especially given the increasing demands placed on fire departments and the need to maximize the effectiveness of training budgets.

However, the adoption of these technologies is not without its challenges. The initial investment in hardware, software, and training can be substantial. Moreover, ensuring that these technologies are user-friendly and accessible to all trainees is crucial. The integration of new technologies requires careful planning and implementation, including addressing potential issues related to data security, privacy, and ethical considerations.

Therefore, a comprehensive strategy is needed to ensure the successful integration of emerging technologies in fire service training. This strategy should involve a phased approach, starting with pilot programs to test the effectiveness of new technologies in a controlled environment. Continuous evaluation and feedback from both instructors and trainees are essential to refine the implementation strategy and identify areas for improvement. Furthermore, collaboration between fire departments, technology providers, and training institutions is crucial to share best practices and ensure that these technologies are deployed effectively and efficiently.

The development and integration of these innovative technologies require a collaborative effort. Fire departments must actively seek partnerships with technology developers, ensuring that the technologies being developed are relevant, practical, and meet the specific needs of the fire service. This collaboration should extend to educational institutions, where research and development can focus on addressing the unique challenges of fire service training. Open-source platforms and sharing of best practices will facilitate broader adoption and ensure affordability.

The potential benefits of embracing these technological advancements are immense. By harnessing the power of AI, ML, VR, and AR, we can create a more effective, engaging, and safer training environment for our firefighters. This, in turn, leads to better-prepared firefighters, improved operational effectiveness, and ultimately, enhanced community safety. The investment in these technologies is not merely an expense; it's an investment in the safety and well-being of our firefighters and the communities they serve. This investment translates directly into better-equipped and more capable personnel, reducing response times and ultimately saving lives.

The future of fire service training is not about replacing human instructors with machines. Instead, it's about empowering instructors with new tools and technologies that enhance their ability to provide effective and engaging training. The human element—the mentorship, the camaraderie, the shared experience—remains irreplaceable. However, the integration of modern technology allows instructors to focus on these crucial elements, freeing them from administrative burdens and providing them with data-driven insights that enhance their teaching effectiveness.

Moreover, the use of these technologies offers opportunities to extend training beyond the traditional classroom setting. Online learning platforms, enhanced by AI-powered adaptive learning modules, can provide ongoing professional development opportunities for firefighters, ensuring that they remain up-to-date with the latest techniques and best practices. This continuous learning approach is essential in an ever-evolving field like fire service, where new threats and challenges are constantly emerging.

Finally, the adoption of these technologies promotes a culture of innovation and continuous improvement within the fire service. By embracing data-driven decision-making and utilizing the latest advancements in technology, fire departments can ensure that their training programs remain at the forefront of effectiveness and safety. This commitment to innovation not only benefits individual firefighters but also enhances the overall efficiency and effectiveness of fire departments, ensuring that they are well-prepared to meet the demands of modern emergencies. The future of fire service training is bright, and the integration of emerging technologies will be instrumental in shaping that future, creating a safer and more effective fire service for generations to come.

The rapid pace of societal and technological change necessitates a similarly agile approach to fire service training. What constituted a significant hazard just a decade ago might be dwarfed by the complexities of today's emergencies, and tomorrow's challenges are likely to be even more unpredictable. Adapting training programs to address these evolving threats is not merely prudent; it's essential for the safety and effectiveness of firefighters and the communities they protect.

One of the most significant shifts in recent years is the increasing prevalence of complex, multi-hazard incidents. No longer are firefighters primarily responding to simple structure fires; they are increasingly facing scenarios involving simultaneous threats like chemical spills, hazardous materials incidents, and active shooter situations. Traditional training programs, often compartmentalized into distinct disciplines, are ill-equipped to address this convergence of hazards. The future of fire service training must embrace a holistic approach, integrating these diverse threats into comprehensive training scenarios that mimic the reality of modern emergencies. This integrated approach should not simply juxtapose different scenarios but rather weave them together, simulating the cascading effects and decision-making challenges that firefighters face in real-world multi-hazard incidents. For example, a training exercise might involve a simulated building collapse caused by a gas explosion, requiring firefighters to manage both structural instability and the dangers of escaping gas in the immediate aftermath.

Beyond the sheer diversity of hazards, the intensity and scale of emergencies are also increasing. Larger buildings, more densely populated urban areas, and increasingly complex infrastructure create scenarios with higher stakes and increased complexity. Training needs to reflect this heightened intensity, pushing firefighters beyond their comfort zones and preparing them to operate effectively under pressure. This necessitates training exercises that simulate the stress, fatigue, and uncertainty inherent in large-scale emergencies, forcing trainees to make critical decisions under immense time constraints. Advanced simulation technologies, such as AI-powered virtual reality, can be invaluable in replicating the dynamic and unpredictable nature of such events, allowing trainees to practice their skills in a safe and controlled environment that nonetheless reflects the pressure of a real-world emergency.

Another crucial area demanding adaptation in training is the increasing prevalence of lithium-ion battery fires. These fires present unique challenges due to their intense heat, unpredictable behavior, and tendency to reignite. Traditional firefighting techniques are often ineffective, requiring specialized training and equipment. Training programs must incorporate specific modules on lithium-ion battery fires, focusing on safe handling procedures, appropriate extinguishing agents, and the importance of thermal imaging cameras in identifying hidden hotspots. This specialized training should go beyond simply explaining the dangers; it should include hands-on practice with specialized equipment and simulated scenarios that allow trainees to develop the necessary skills and decision-making capabilities to effectively manage these increasingly common and dangerous incidents. Practical exercises focusing on the unique thermal properties and the potential for reignition are crucial in this context, ensuring firefighters are adequately prepared for the challenges these batteries present.

The rise of electric vehicles (EVs) presents similar challenges. The high-voltage systems within EVs pose significant risks to firefighters, and the materials used in their construction can lead to complex fire behaviors. Training programs must include dedicated sessions on EV safety, covering topics such as high-voltage isolation procedures, appropriate firefighting techniques for EV batteries, and the use of specialized tools and equipment. Interactive simulations replicating real-world scenarios, including potential hazards associated with high-voltage systems, could drastically improve training effectiveness. Emphasis should be placed on safe handling of high-voltage components and the use of specialized equipment designed to mitigate risks. The training should cover procedures for disconnection of power sources, strategies to manage thermal runaway in EV batteries, and protocols for handling and extinguishing fires within these vehicles.

Beyond technological advancements, social and environmental changes also demand an evolving training approach. Climate change is leading to more frequent and intense weather events, such as wildfires, floods, and hurricanes. Training programs need to include modules on disaster response and preparedness, focusing on techniques for working in challenging environmental conditions, coordinating with other agencies, and providing support to affected communities. This includes training on advanced search and rescue techniques within disaster zones, strategies for providing assistance in flooded areas, and establishing safe operating procedures during extreme weather events. The focus should be on developing the resilience and adaptability needed to handle the increasingly intense and complex emergencies brought on by climate change.

The changing demographics of our communities also require adaptation in training. Firefighters need to be prepared to respond to a diverse range of individuals with varying needs and vulnerabilities. Training should include modules on cultural sensitivity, effective communication with diverse populations, and techniques for providing appropriate care to individuals with disabilities or special needs. The ability to communicate effectively and build rapport with individuals from different backgrounds is essential for ensuring a safe and effective response during emergencies. Simulated scenarios reflecting the diverse range of community members and potential challenges during emergency response can greatly improve the ability to handle stressful real-world scenarios.

Furthermore, the integration of technology into training must adapt to meet these evolving threats. AI-powered simulations can be customized to reflect specific hazards, creating training scenarios that replicate the complexities of real-world emergencies. This can include simulating the behavior of different types of hazardous materials, the dynamics of complex building collapses, or the unpredictable nature of extreme weather events. Virtual reality and augmented reality can offer even more immersive and engaging training experiences. Through these technologies, firefighters can practice their skills in a safe and controlled environment, building confidence and expertise in handling diverse and complex emergencies. The possibilities are extensive, and adapting training programs to leverage these technologies will ensure that firefighters are adequately prepared to meet future challenges.

In conclusion, the future of fire service training rests on the ability to adapt to a constantly evolving landscape of threats and hazards. A holistic approach that integrates diverse disciplines, simulates high-intensity scenarios, and incorporates specialized training for emerging hazards is paramount. The effective integration of advanced technology will play a key role in this adaptation, providing tools for realistic simulations, personalized training, and ongoing professional development. By embracing innovation and adapting to the ever-changing demands of the fire service, we can ensure that our firefighters are well-prepared to protect our communities for years to come. The investment in this continuous adaptation is not just a cost; it is an investment in the safety and well-being of our firefighters and the communities they serve, ensuring effective and efficient response to an ever-changing range of emergency situations. The ultimate goal is to build a safer and more resilient future for all.

The evolving landscape of fire service demands a proactive approach to training, one that anticipates future challenges rather than simply reacting to them. This requires a fundamental shift from traditional pedagogical methods towards a more dynamic, adaptive, and technology-integrated training paradigm. We must move beyond the confines of static lectures and rote memorization, embracing instead a future-ready approach that fosters critical thinking, problem-solving skills, and adaptability in the face of unprecedented emergencies.

One key aspect of developing future-ready firefighters lies in embracing technological advancements. The integration of sophisticated simulation technologies, such as virtual reality (VR) and augmented reality (AR), offers unparalleled opportunities to create immersive and engaging training environments. VR allows trainees to experience realistic simulations of hazardous situations – from high-rise building fires and hazardous materials spills to complex urban search and rescue operations – without the risks associated with real-world scenarios. This immersive experience fosters a deeper understanding of situational awareness, decision-making under pressure, and the practical application of firefighting techniques. Trainees can repeatedly practice complex maneuvers, refine their strategies, and learn from their mistakes in a safe and controlled environment, building confidence and competence before facing real-world emergencies.

Augmented reality, on the other hand, overlays digital information onto the real world, providing firefighters with real-time data and guidance during training exercises. For instance, AR can be used to project thermal images onto a burning structure, highlighting hotspots and potential hazards that might otherwise be invisible to the naked eye. This technology enhances situational awareness and facilitates more effective decision-making, particularly in complex or obscured environments. The use of AR can also enhance the effectiveness of practical training exercises by providing immediate feedback on performance, allowing trainees to identify areas for improvement and refine their skills. The integration of both VR and AR creates a powerful synergy, allowing for a more comprehensive and engaging training experience that blends the immersive nature of virtual environments with the practicality of real-world application.

Furthermore, the incorporation of artificial intelligence (AI) in fire service training is poised to revolutionize the way we prepare firefighters for future challenges. AI-powered simulations can create dynamic and unpredictable scenarios that mirror the complexities of real-world emergencies. These simulations can adapt to the trainees' actions, providing personalized challenges and feedback that cater to individual learning styles and skill levels. AI can also be used to analyze trainee performance, identifying areas of strength and weakness and providing targeted recommendations for improvement. This data-driven approach to training ensures that resources are allocated efficiently and that firefighters receive the specific training they need to excel in their roles. Moreover, AI can assist in developing and adapting training programs based on real-world incident data, ensuring that training remains relevant and effective in addressing evolving threats.

Beyond technological advancements, developing future-ready firefighters requires a fundamental shift in pedagogical approaches. We must move away from traditional lecture-based training and embrace more interactive and engaging methods that cater to the diverse learning styles of modern recruits. This includes incorporating problem-based learning, where trainees are presented with complex scenarios and encouraged to develop their own solutions through critical thinking and collaboration. This approach fosters creativity, independent thinking and a deeper understanding of the underlying principles of firefighting. Moreover, it encourages a sense of ownership and responsibility, crucial for effective leadership and teamwork within the fire service.

The integration of gamification techniques can also significantly enhance the engagement and effectiveness of fire service training. By incorporating game-like elements, such as points, rewards, and challenges, we can make learning more enjoyable and motivating. This can include the use of interactive simulations, competitive exercises, and team-based challenges, which foster collaboration and create a sense of accomplishment. Gamification not only enhances the learning experience but also helps build confidence, resilience, and teamwork skills, essential attributes for effective firefighters.

Equally important is the need for continuous professional development. The fire service is a constantly evolving field, with new technologies, techniques, and hazards emerging regularly. Future-ready firefighters must be committed to lifelong learning, continuously updating their skills and knowledge to stay abreast of the latest advancements. This requires a robust system of ongoing training and professional development, including regular refresher courses, specialized workshops, and access to online learning resources. Investing in continuous professional development not only enhances the skills and knowledge of individual firefighters but also ensures the overall effectiveness and safety of the fire service as a whole.

Furthermore, fostering a culture of safety and risk management is paramount in developing future-ready firefighters. This involves integrating safety protocols into every aspect of training, emphasizing the importance of risk assessment, personal protective equipment (PPE), and safe operating procedures. Trainees must be instilled with a strong sense of safety awareness, and they must understand that safety is not just a priority but a fundamental aspect of effective firefighting. Regular safety briefings, simulations of hazardous situations, and post-incident analysis sessions will help build and maintain this safety culture.

Finally, developing future-ready firefighters is not merely about equipping them with the technical skills and knowledge; it is also about fostering a sense of purpose, compassion, and leadership. Firefighters often face emotionally challenging situations, requiring them to display resilience, empathy, and the ability to provide support to individuals in crisis. Therefore, training must incorporate elements of emotional intelligence, stress management, and crisis intervention. This may include sessions on communication skills, ethical decision-making, and cultural sensitivity, enabling firefighters to connect with and serve diverse communities effectively.

In conclusion, developing future-ready firefighters requires a comprehensive and forward-thinking approach that integrates technology, innovative pedagogical methods, and a strong emphasis on safety and continuous professional development. By embracing these principles, we can prepare firefighters not only for the challenges of today but also for the ever-evolving demands of tomorrow, ensuring their safety, effectiveness, and the well-being of the communities they serve. The investment in such a proactive training approach is not merely an expense; it is a crucial investment in the safety and security of our future.

The preceding discussion focused on technological advancements and pedagogical shifts in fire service training. However, preparing firefighters for the future also necessitates a deep consideration of sustainability and environmental responsibility. The fire service, by its very nature, interacts extensively with the environment, often in destructive ways. Fires themselves are inherently damaging, but our response to them can also have significant environmental consequences. Therefore, integrating sustainability into fire service training is not merely a desirable add-on; it's a critical component of preparing effective and responsible firefighters for the challenges ahead.

One crucial aspect is the reduction of the fire service's environmental footprint. This begins with the training facilities themselves. Designing and operating training centers with sustainability in mind is a crucial step. This includes adopting energy-efficient building designs, utilizing renewable energy sources such as solar panels and wind turbines, and implementing water conservation measures. The use of sustainable building materials, minimizing waste generation during construction and operation, and proper recycling and waste management programs are all essential elements of a green training facility. Furthermore, the curriculum should incorporate instruction on the environmental impact of firefighting activities, including the use of water, foam, and other extinguishing agents. Trainees should understand the environmental consequences of these substances and learn environmentally responsible techniques to mitigate their impact.

Moving beyond the training facilities, we must examine the environmental impacts of fire suppression techniques. The overuse of water in firefighting can lead to significant water depletion, particularly in drought-prone regions. Fire service training should emphasize water conservation techniques, such as using precise water application methods, employing alternative extinguishing agents where appropriate, and effectively managing water runoff to prevent contamination. This includes instruction on the proper use of specialized equipment, such as high-pressure fog nozzles, which can significantly reduce water consumption while maintaining fire suppression effectiveness. The training should also cover the ecological impact of different extinguishing agents, including the potential harm to aquatic life and the long-term effects on soil and vegetation.

The use of foam, while effective in suppressing certain types of fires, can have significant environmental consequences. Fluorinated fire-fighting foams, in particular, contain PFAS (per- and polyfluoroalkyl substances), which are persistent, bioaccumulative, and toxic substances that can contaminate water sources and pose health risks to humans and wildlife. Training should emphasize the responsible handling and disposal of these foams, along with exploring and utilizing more environmentally friendly alternatives whenever feasible. This includes training on the proper techniques for applying foam, minimizing over-application, and implementing robust containment and cleanup protocols to minimize environmental contamination. Exploring and practicing the use of alternative, more sustainable extinguishing agents should also be a key component of the training curriculum.

The sustainability focus shouldn't be limited to extinguishing agents. The fire service uses a significant amount of fuel in its vehicles and equipment. Training should incorporate instruction on fuel-efficient driving techniques, the proper maintenance of equipment to optimize fuel efficiency, and the exploration of alternative fuel sources for fire service vehicles, such as electric or hybrid vehicles. Furthermore, the fire service can explore the use of sustainable materials in the production and maintenance of its equipment. This includes exploring recycled materials, bio-based materials, and other sustainable alternatives in the manufacturing process.

Beyond the direct environmental impact of firefighting operations, the training program can also incorporate environmental awareness and preparedness. Firefighters are often the first responders to environmental emergencies, such as hazardous materials spills, wildfires, and other incidents that threaten the environment. Training should equip firefighters with the knowledge and skills needed to effectively respond to such emergencies, minimizing environmental damage and protecting human health and safety. This includes training on hazardous materials identification and handling, proper cleanup techniques, and environmental monitoring procedures.

Furthermore, the training program should emphasize the importance of community engagement and environmental stewardship. Firefighters play a critical role in educating the public about fire safety and environmental protection. Training should include sessions on public education and outreach strategies, enabling firefighters to effectively communicate environmental messages and engage communities in protecting the environment. This can include community events, workshops, and presentations focusing on fire prevention, environmental responsibility, and preparedness for natural disasters.

The integration of sustainability into fire service training is not merely a matter of environmental responsibility; it's also about enhancing operational efficiency and reducing costs. By adopting more sustainable practices, fire departments can reduce their energy consumption, water usage, and waste generation, leading to significant cost savings in the long run. Furthermore, adopting environmentally friendly practices can enhance the department's public image and strengthen its relationship with the community.

The future of the fire service is inextricably linked to the environment. By proactively integrating sustainability into fire service training, we are not only preparing firefighters for the challenges of tomorrow, but also ensuring the long-term sustainability of the fire service itself. This comprehensive approach will create a more responsible and resilient fire service, equipped to protect both lives and the environment. This commitment to sustainability is not merely a trend; it's a fundamental shift in how we envision and operate the fire service in a world increasingly impacted by climate change and environmental degradation. By embracing this responsibility, we are ensuring the long-term viability and effectiveness of the fire service, preparing future generations of firefighters to serve their communities while protecting the very planet they are sworn to protect. This commitment extends beyond merely reducing our environmental impact; it signifies a profound transformation, embedding environmental consciousness as an integral element of firefighting strategy and operational excellence. The ultimate goal is to equip firefighters with the knowledge, skills, and attitude necessary to become true environmental stewards, capable of responding effectively and sustainably to the challenges of the 21st century and beyond.

Building upon the crucial integration of sustainability into fire service training, we now turn our attention to another vital aspect of future-proofing the profession: fostering robust collaboration and knowledge sharing across different fire departments. In an increasingly interconnected world, the siloed approach to training, common in the past, is no longer sufficient. The sharing of best practices, innovative techniques, and lessons learned is essential for optimizing training effectiveness and ensuring that all firefighters, regardless of their department's size or location, receive the highest quality instruction.

Effective knowledge sharing is not merely about disseminating information; it's about building a collective learning environment where departments can learn from each other's successes and failures. This requires a fundamental shift in mindset, moving away from a culture of competition towards one of mutual support and collaboration. Such a transition fosters an environment where departments are comfortable sharing their training materials, methodologies, and even their mistakes. Open communication and transparency are vital in this process, allowing departments to learn from each other's experiences and avoid repeating costly errors.

One avenue for achieving this is through the establishment of regional or national training networks. These networks can facilitate the sharing of training resources, best practices, and innovative training technologies. For instance, a department that has developed a particularly effective training program for hazardous materials incidents can share their curriculum and materials with other departments in the network, saving time, resources, and effort. Likewise, departments that have experienced challenges in a particular area of training can share those experiences to help others avoid similar pitfalls. These networks should not just be platforms for the dissemination of information but also for fostering dialogue and discussion, enabling departments to learn from each other's unique perspectives and experiences.

Regular training exchanges between departments can also significantly enhance knowledge sharing. These exchanges can involve sending instructors or trainees to other departments to observe and participate in their training programs. This hands-on experience provides valuable insights into different training methodologies and allows participants to learn from the strengths and weaknesses of different approaches. These exchanges can also foster stronger relationships between departments, leading to increased collaboration and mutual support. Furthermore, these exchanges should actively incorporate feedback mechanisms to ensure continuous improvement and adaptation of training methods.

Technology plays a crucial role in facilitating knowledge sharing across departments. The use of online platforms and digital repositories allows departments to easily share training materials, videos, and other resources. These platforms can also facilitate communication and collaboration among training staff, enabling them to share ideas, discuss challenges, and provide support to one another. The use of virtual reality (VR) and augmented reality (AR) technologies is also transforming training, allowing departments to simulate real-world scenarios and provide immersive training experiences. Sharing access to these technologies across departments can significantly enhance the quality and effectiveness of training.

Furthermore, the development of standardized training curricula across departments can ensure consistency and improve the overall quality of training. While it's vital to maintain flexibility to adapt to specific local needs, establishing core competencies and a standardized framework can ensure that all firefighters receive training in essential skills and knowledge, regardless of their department. This ensures consistency across jurisdictions and simplifies the process of transferring firefighters between different departments. This standardization facilitates seamless integration and minimizes potential gaps in training, improving interoperability and overall safety.

Beyond the technical aspects, creating a culture that prioritizes knowledge sharing requires a significant shift in departmental attitudes and practices. Leadership plays a crucial role in establishing this culture by explicitly valuing collaboration and encouraging open communication among training staff and firefighters. Departmental policies should reflect this commitment, incentivizing knowledge sharing and providing the resources necessary for departments to participate in training networks and exchanges. This includes allocating budgets for travel, training materials, and the development of collaborative online platforms. Crucially, a culture of trust and mutual respect is paramount; departments must feel safe in sharing both successes and challenges without fear of judgment or repercussions.

Incentivizing knowledge sharing can also be achieved through various methods. Rewarding departments that actively participate in training networks and exchanges, recognizing outstanding instructors who share their expertise, and showcasing successful collaborations through publications or presentations can all encourage active participation. This positive reinforcement can create a positive feedback loop, further encouraging the sharing of best practices and fostering a more collaborative training environment.

The impact of collaboration and knowledge sharing extends beyond individual departments; it benefits the entire fire service community. By working together, departments can develop more effective training programs, improve firefighter safety, and enhance the overall effectiveness of emergency response. This collective learning approach also contributes to advancements in the field, as innovations and improvements in training are rapidly disseminated and adopted across the community. This synergy leads to a more efficient and effective fire service as a whole.

The sharing of information is not limited to training techniques. Departments can also collaborate on research projects, focusing on improving firefighter health and safety, developing new firefighting technologies, and advancing understanding of fire dynamics. Collaboration on these research initiatives fosters a stronger understanding of emerging challenges and allows for the development of more informed and effective training programs. The collaborative analysis of data gathered from fire incidents, training exercises, and research studies can provide valuable insights into improving safety protocols and developing more targeted and effective training.

Moreover, the collaborative spirit should extend to the sharing of resources and equipment. Departments with access to specialized equipment or training facilities can make these resources available to other departments, maximizing the use of resources and minimizing costs. This sharing of resources not only reduces expenses but also allows departments with limited resources to access advanced training and equipment that would otherwise be unavailable. This collaborative approach fosters a sense of community and shared responsibility across all departments.

In conclusion, the future of fire service training hinges on a strong commitment to collaboration and knowledge sharing. By fostering a culture of openness, trust, and mutual support among departments, we can significantly improve the quality, effectiveness, and consistency of training across the fire service. This collective learning approach not only enhances the skills and knowledge of individual firefighters but also strengthens the overall resilience and effectiveness of the fire service as a whole, preparing it to face the complex challenges of the future. This is more than simply a training strategy; it is a paradigm shift in how we view the fire service, transforming it into a collaborative, interconnected network focused on shared growth, continuous improvement, and ultimately, enhancing the safety and wellbeing of both firefighters and the communities they serve.

Chapter 13: Conclusion and Call to Action

This book has explored a transformative approach to fire service recruit training, prioritizing the "why" before the "how." We've challenged the traditional, lecture-heavy methodology, advocating instead for a more engaging, experiential learning process deeply rooted in understanding the fundamental principles behind firefighting techniques. This shift is not merely a pedagogical preference; it's a necessity driven by the evolving learning styles of modern recruits and the urgent need to optimize training investment for peak performance and long-term success.

The core argument rests on the understanding that recruits, shaped by readily available online information and diverse learning experiences, respond better to a methodology that explains the rationale and significance of each procedure before diving into the technical execution. This approach moves beyond rote memorization and fosters a deeper comprehension of the underlying principles, leading to enhanced retention, better problem-solving skills, and ultimately, increased proficiency in real-world scenarios.

We've examined the limitations of the "death by PowerPoint" style of instruction, highlighting how passive learning fails to engage the recruits and often leads to poor retention and lack of motivation. Instead, we've championed a blend of interactive lectures, hands-on simulations, and scenario-based training, incorporating elements of adult learning theory to maximize effectiveness. Effective instruction requires recognizing the adult learner's unique characteristics: their self-direction, experience, and motivation. The training needs to resonate with their life experiences and professional goals, making the learning relevant and purposeful. This requires instructors to move beyond simple information delivery and become facilitators of learning, guiding recruits towards self-discovery and mastery of the subject matter.

The book delved extensively into practical strategies designed to boost student engagement and maintain attention. These included incorporating real-world examples, leveraging storytelling techniques to connect with recruits on a personal level, utilizing varied teaching methods to cater to different learning styles (visual, auditory, kinesthetic), and designing training exercises that challenge recruits to apply their knowledge in simulated, high-pressure environments. Regular feedback, formative assessment throughout the learning process, and providing opportunities for self-reflection are critical for maximizing learning outcomes. These practices not only enhance the learning experience but also cultivate a more positive and supportive learning environment, helping to foster a sense of camaraderie and teamwork amongst recruits.

A significant emphasis was placed on the crucial role of instructors in shaping the next generation of firefighters. Effective instructors are not simply disseminators of information; they are mentors, role models, and sources of inspiration. They must create a learning atmosphere characterized by trust, mutual respect, and open communication, encouraging questions, embracing feedback, and fostering a culture of continuous improvement. This involves understanding the recruits' individual learning styles and adapting the teaching methods accordingly, employing effective communication strategies, and fostering a learning environment that is both challenging and supportive.

The investment fire departments make in recruit training is substantial. Therefore, optimizing the training process to ensure that recruits acquire the necessary knowledge and skills is paramount for public safety and operational efficiency. This necessitates a continuous evaluation and refinement of training programs, incorporating feedback from recruits, instructors, and operational personnel to ensure that the training remains relevant, effective, and aligned with the evolving demands of the profession. Regular updates to training materials and methodologies are crucial to keep pace with technological advancements and changes in firefighting tactics.

Furthermore, we discussed the critical importance of incorporating sustainability principles into fire service training. This involves not only environmental considerations, such as reducing the environmental impact of training exercises, but also the sustainability of the training programs themselves—ensuring their longevity and adaptability to changing needs. This requires a thoughtful approach to curriculum design, resource allocation, and the adoption of innovative teaching methods. This also includes consideration for the long-term well-being of firefighters, promoting healthy lifestyles, mental fitness, and injury prevention strategies. The sustainability of the fire service is not just about environmental considerations, but also about the sustained health and effectiveness of its personnel.

The final chapters highlighted the vital role of inter-departmental collaboration and knowledge sharing in elevating the standard of fire service training. By moving beyond a siloed approach, departments can learn from each other's successes and challenges, leading to improved training programs, enhanced firefighter safety, and better overall emergency response capabilities. This requires a shift in mindset, fostering a culture of openness and mutual support among departments, encouraging the sharing of best practices, training materials, and lessons learned. This collaborative spirit enhances the profession as a whole, benefiting both individual firefighters and the communities they serve. This includes actively sharing resources, both physical and intellectual, and establishing collaborative networks that allow for the cross-pollination of ideas and techniques.

Effective collaboration requires the establishment of communication channels for sharing best practices and lessons learned, the development of standardized training curricula (while acknowledging the need for local adaptation), and the utilization of technology to facilitate remote collaboration and access to shared resources. This can include establishing online platforms for the sharing of training materials, videos, and other resources, utilizing virtual and augmented reality technologies for immersive training experiences, and creating opportunities for instructors and trainees to participate in training exchanges and collaborative research projects.

In summary, this book has presented a comprehensive framework for transforming fire service recruit training. By prioritizing the "why," emphasizing experiential learning, fostering a culture of continuous improvement, incorporating sustainability principles, and embracing collaboration, fire departments can significantly improve the quality of their training programs, leading to more competent, confident, and well-prepared firefighters. This not only enhances firefighter safety and operational effectiveness but also creates a more engaging and fulfilling profession, attracting and retaining the best candidates and inspiring a new generation of dedicated and highly skilled firefighters who are well-equipped to face the evolving challenges of the modern fire service. The success of this approach relies on a sustained commitment from leadership, instructors, and trainees alike. It is a continuous journey of improvement, adaptation, and collaboration, ultimately aimed at enhancing the safety and well-being of both firefighters and the communities they protect. The investment in effective training is an investment in the future of the fire service, ensuring its ability to respond effectively to the ever-changing challenges and demands of the 21st century. The ultimate goal is not just to train firefighters, but to cultivate a passionate, skilled, and resilient workforce dedicated to public service and committed to excellence. This paradigm shift prioritizes not just the techniques of firefighting, but the development of critical thinking, problem-solving abilities, and above all, a deep understanding of the inherent value and responsibility of this vital profession. The future of the fire service depends on it.

The preceding chapters have laid out a compelling case for a revolutionary shift in fire service recruit training, prioritizing the "why" behind firefighting techniques before the "how." This approach, rooted in modern pedagogical principles and tailored to the learning styles of today's recruits, yields significant benefits, culminating in more proficient, confident, and engaged firefighters. But the success of this transformative approach hinges on a crucial factor: a robust commitment to investing in high-quality firefighter training. This isn't merely about budgetary allocation; it's a strategic investment in public safety, operational efficiency, and the long-term viability of the fire service itself.

The financial commitment to training is substantial, encompassing salaries for instructors, development and maintenance of training facilities, procurement of training equipment (including sophisticated simulators and virtual reality tools), the costs associated with developing and updating training materials, and the ongoing professional development of instructors themselves. This investment, however significant, pales in comparison to the potential costs of inadequate training. Underprepared firefighters are at a greater risk of injury or fatality, leading to increased worker's compensation claims, potential lawsuits, and the emotional toll on fellow firefighters and their families. Furthermore, inadequately trained personnel may compromise the effectiveness of emergency responses, leading to increased property damage, environmental hazards, and even loss of life within the communities served.

The return on investment in effective training is multifaceted. Well-trained firefighters are more efficient in emergency response, leading to quicker containment of fires, better rescue operations, and ultimately, a reduction in property damage and loss of life. Their improved skills also contribute to minimizing injuries within the fire service itself, a critical factor considering the inherent risks associated with the profession. This translates directly into lower healthcare costs and reduced worker's compensation payouts. Beyond immediate operational efficiency, investing in high-quality training contributes to the long-term sustainability of the fire service. It attracts and retains talented recruits, fostering a more skilled and motivated workforce. A positive training experience not only instills a sense of pride and professionalism but also enhances morale and fosters a sense of camaraderie among firefighters.

This positive feedback loop enhances retention rates, reducing the costs associated with recruitment and training new recruits. In an era of increasing budgetary constraints, efficient training programs become crucial for sustaining operational capabilities and maintaining public safety standards. Investing in training also helps fire departments stay abreast of the latest technologies, techniques, and best practices within the profession. The rapid pace of technological advancement in firefighting necessitates continuous updating of training programs to ensure firefighters are equipped to handle the challenges of modern emergencies. This includes familiarization with new equipment, evolving firefighting tactics, and the integration of emerging technologies such as drones, thermal imaging cameras, and advanced communication systems.

Furthermore, the investment in training transcends the purely technical aspects of firefighting. Effective training programs also emphasize the development of critical thinking skills, problem-solving abilities, and effective teamwork. These soft skills are invaluable in high-pressure situations, allowing firefighters to adapt quickly to unforeseen circumstances and work effectively as part of a cohesive unit. The development of strong leadership qualities within the ranks of firefighters, fostered through mentorship programs and leadership training, contributes to improved operational efficiency and enhanced morale within the team. The investment in building well-rounded, capable firefighters extends far beyond the immediate requirements of emergency response, contributing to the overall well-being and resilience of the fire service as a whole.

This investment also extends to the importance of promoting a culture of continuous learning and professional development within the fire service. Firefighters should not view training as a one-time event, but rather as an ongoing process of skill enhancement and knowledge acquisition throughout their career. This requires departments to provide opportunities for ongoing training, including advanced training courses, specialized certifications, and access to online learning

252.

resources. Investing in professional development not only enhances the individual firefighter's skills but also raises the overall competency level of the entire department. This continuous learning approach helps to maintain a highly skilled workforce, ensuring that departments remain prepared to face the ever-evolving challenges of the fire service.

The emphasis on investing in firefighter training also extends to the well-being of the firefighters themselves. A comprehensive training program should incorporate strategies for promoting physical and mental health, injury prevention, and stress management. This includes providing access to physical fitness programs, mental health resources, and peer support networks. Investing in the health and well-being of firefighters is not only a moral imperative, but also a pragmatic one. It reduces the risk of injuries, improves operational effectiveness, and enhances morale, ultimately resulting in a more sustainable and effective fire service. This includes recognizing and addressing issues such as PTSD and other mental health challenges that are uniquely prevalent within this high-stress profession. By fostering a supportive and caring environment, fire departments demonstrate a commitment to the well-being of their personnel, improving retention and fostering a stronger sense of camaraderie.

It's critical to acknowledge that the investment in firefighter training is not simply a cost, but a strategic investment with a substantial return. The benefits extend far beyond the immediate financial implications, encompassing improved public safety, enhanced operational efficiency, a more resilient workforce, and the fostering of a positive and sustainable fire service culture. It's an investment in the future of the fire service itself, ensuring its ability to adapt to evolving challenges and continue to effectively serve the communities it protects. This holistic approach, encompassing not only technical skills but also the development of critical thinking, teamwork, leadership, and well-being, leads to a more highly skilled, engaged, and resilient firefighting force.

Moreover, the effective utilization of resources is paramount. A well-structured training program should optimize resources to maximize the learning outcomes. This means careful planning of training schedules, efficient use of training facilities and equipment, and the strategic development of training materials that are both cost-effective and impactful. The use of technology can greatly enhance this efficiency, through the utilization of online learning platforms, interactive simulations, and virtual reality training environments. These tools offer cost-effective and accessible alternatives to traditional, resource-intensive training methods, allowing for a greater reach and increased training opportunities.

Finally, a successful investment in training is not simply a matter of financial allocation but also requires a cultural shift within fire departments. Leadership must champion a culture of learning, providing the necessary support, resources, and recognition for firefighters who actively pursue professional development. This involves creating a training environment that fosters continuous learning, celebrates success, and encourages feedback and continuous improvement. Effective communication is also paramount, ensuring that both recruits and experienced firefighters understand the value of training and the department's commitment to ongoing professional development.

In conclusion, the investment in high-quality fire service training is not an expense, but rather a critical investment in public safety, operational efficiency, and the long-term sustainability of the fire service itself. It is an investment in the well-being of firefighters, fostering a more skilled, engaged, and resilient workforce capable of facing the ever-evolving challenges of the 21st century. This commitment must be unwavering, reflecting a deep understanding of the vital role firefighters play in protecting lives and property. By prioritizing training and fostering a culture of continuous learning, fire departments can ensure the safety of their personnel, optimize operational efficiency, and ultimately, contribute significantly to the well-being of the communities they serve. This is not simply about ensuring proficiency in extinguishing fires; it's about building a resilient, capable, and passionate fire service capable of meeting the challenges of tomorrow. The investment in training is an investment in a safer, more secure future for all.

The previous discussion highlighted the critical importance of investing in high-quality fire service training, emphasizing its multifaceted returns. However, simply allocating resources is insufficient; we must also embrace innovation and change in our approach. The fire service, like any dynamic profession, must continually adapt to meet evolving challenges. This necessitates a fundamental shift in our training methodologies, moving beyond traditional, often outdated, practices.

One significant area for improvement lies in leveraging technology. While traditional methods, such as lectures and hands-on drills, remain essential, they can be significantly enhanced through the integration of technology. Virtual reality (VR) and augmented reality (AR) simulations offer unparalleled opportunities for immersive training experiences. Recruits can practice complex scenarios, such as high-rise rescues or hazardous material incidents, in a safe and controlled environment, without risking injury or damage to equipment. These simulations can replicate the stress and complexity of real-world emergencies, allowing recruits to develop critical decision-making skills and build confidence in their abilities.

Furthermore, online learning platforms offer unparalleled flexibility and accessibility. They allow recruits to learn at their own pace, revisit materials as needed, and access supplemental resources. This personalized approach caters to diverse learning styles and accommodates the busy schedules of modern recruits, enhancing the overall training effectiveness. Interactive modules, incorporating videos, quizzes, and simulations, can make learning more engaging and less reliant on passive lectures. This modern approach not only enhances knowledge retention but also fosters a more positive learning experience.

Beyond technology, we must embrace innovative pedagogical approaches. The shift from a purely knowledge-based curriculum to one that prioritizes skills development and critical thinking is crucial. Problem-based learning (PBL), where recruits tackle real-world scenarios and develop solutions collaboratively, fosters deeper understanding and enhances problem-solving abilities. This approach moves away from rote memorization and encourages a deeper engagement with the material, resulting in more adaptable and effective firefighters. Incorporating simulations and role-playing exercises allows recruits to experience the challenges of firefighting in a safe environment, developing essential skills and building confidence.

Moreover, fostering a culture of continuous learning and professional development is paramount. Firefighters should view training not as a one-time event, but as an ongoing process of skill enhancement and knowledge acquisition throughout their career. This requires departments to provide ongoing opportunities for training, including advanced courses, specialized certifications, and access to online resources. Regular professional development sessions focusing on leadership, teamwork, and crisis management further enhance their abilities, creating a culture of constant improvement.

This continual learning process isn't simply about updating technical skills; it's about nurturing adaptability and critical thinking. The fire service landscape is ever-shifting, with new hazards, techniques, and technologies continually emerging. Firefighters need to be equipped not just with the skills of today, but the capacity to learn and adapt to the challenges of tomorrow. Incorporating scenario-based training, where recruits analyze and respond to unexpected events, is crucial for building adaptability and resilience.

The shift towards innovative training also demands a change in instructional methodology. The traditional "death by PowerPoint" approach, characterized by lengthy lectures and passive learning, must be replaced with more interactive and engaging methods. Incorporating active learning techniques, such as group discussions, hands-on activities, and simulations, enhances engagement and retention. This modern approach recognizes that learning is an active process, requiring participation and critical thinking. Instructors should become facilitators of learning, guiding recruits towards deeper understanding rather than simply delivering information.

This shift also calls for the creation of a supportive and inclusive learning environment. This means fostering open communication, encouraging questions and feedback, and creating a culture of mutual respect and collaboration. Recruits should feel comfortable expressing their thoughts and concerns, knowing that their input is valued. This positive and encouraging environment is essential for building confidence, promoting effective learning, and creating a sense of camaraderie among recruits. A collaborative learning atmosphere also fosters a supportive environment conducive to sharing knowledge and experiences.

The adoption of innovative training methods also requires a commitment to ongoing evaluation and improvement. Regular assessments of training programs are necessary to gauge their effectiveness and identify areas for improvement. This could include collecting feedback from recruits, monitoring performance data, and analyzing incident reports to identify areas where training can be strengthened. This continuous cycle of evaluation and improvement is essential for ensuring that training programs remain relevant, effective, and aligned with the needs of the fire service.

Moreover, effective training must consider the diverse needs of learners. Not all recruits learn in the same way. Some may be visual learners, while others prefer hands-on experiences. A multifaceted approach that accommodates diverse learning
styles is essential for maximizing the impact of training. This could involve incorporating different instructional methods, utilizing a variety of learning resources, and providing individualized support to learners who require additional assistance.

Crucially, embracing innovation requires a cultural shift within the fire service. Leadership must champion this change, providing the necessary support, resources, and recognition for instructors who adopt new methods. This includes providing access to professional development opportunities for instructors, encouraging experimentation with new technologies and pedagogical approaches, and celebrating the successes of innovative training initiatives. This requires fostering a culture where innovation is not only accepted but actively encouraged and celebrated.

Finally, this call to embrace innovation is not a rejection of traditional methods but rather a call for their enhancement and integration with modern approaches. The core principles of firefighting remain vital, but the way in which we teach and learn these principles must adapt to the changing landscape of the 21st century. By embracing innovation and change, we can ensure that our fire service recruits are equipped with the skills, knowledge, and resilience to meet the challenges of tomorrow, safeguarding both themselves and the communities they serve. It's about building a future-ready fire service, capable of adapting to unforeseen challenges and maintaining the highest standards of safety and effectiveness. This requires a dedication to continuous improvement, a willingness to experiment, and a commitment to fostering a culture of learning and innovation within every fire service department. The investment in this transformation will undoubtedly lead to a more proficient, adaptable, and resilient fire service, capable of meeting the demands of the future with confidence and skill.

This concluding chapter has emphasized the transformative potential of prioritizing the "why" in fire service recruit training. The shift towards a more engaging, technologically integrated, and pedagogically sound approach isn't merely an upgrade; it's a fundamental reimagining of how we equip the next generation of firefighters. To further explore these concepts and solidify your understanding, we offer a range of resources and further reading materials categorized for ease of access.

I. Foundational Texts on Adult Learning and Pedagogy:

This section focuses on the core principles of adult education, critical for understanding how best to engage and instruct adult learners in the fire service context. These aren't solely firefighting manuals; rather, they provide a theoretical framework to inform your training strategies.

Malcolm Knowles' The Adult Learner: Knowles' seminal work remains a cornerstone in the field of adult education. His principles of andragogy—the art and science of helping adults learn—directly address the unique characteristics of adult learners, their self-concept, prior experience, readiness to learn, orientation to learning, and motivation. Understanding Knowles' framework provides a robust foundation for designing effective training programs that resonate with the experience and expectations of fire service recruits. Applying Knowles' concepts can significantly enhance the effectiveness of your training, moving beyond simple knowledge transfer to fostering a deeper understanding and internalization of firefighting principles.

Educause's Seven Principles for Good Practice in Undergraduate Education: While focused on undergraduate education, these principles surprisingly translate well to the fire service training context. They emphasize active learning, prompt feedback, time on task, and the development of learning communities—all essential for creating a dynamic and effective training environment for recruits. Applying these principles can help to transform your training sessions from passive lectures into interactive experiences that foster deeper engagement and improved knowledge retention.

Chickering and Gamson's Seven Principles for Good Practice in Undergraduate Education: This work complements the Educause principles, offering further insights into creating a supportive learning environment that fosters collaboration and critical thinking. The emphasis on active learning, collaborative learning, and timely feedback are crucial components of effective fire service training. It's particularly relevant to the shift away from traditional lecture-based methodologies.

II. Technology Integration in Fire Service Training:

This section delves into the practical applications of technology in enhancing fire service training, offering resources on the selection, implementation, and effective use of technological tools.

National Fire Protection Association (NFPA) publications on training technology: The NFPA publishes numerous standards and guidelines related to fire service training, many of which incorporate the use of technology. These resources offer valuable insights into best practices, safety regulations, and the integration of technology into various aspects of fire service training, from virtual reality simulations to online learning platforms. Staying up-to-date with NFPA publications is crucial for ensuring your training programs align with the latest safety standards and technological advancements.

Case studies on the use of virtual reality (VR) and augmented reality (AR) in fire service training: Several organizations and institutions have conducted research on the effectiveness of VR and AR in fire service training. These case studies offer valuable insights into the practical applications of these technologies, the challenges encountered during implementation, and the measurable outcomes achieved. Studying these case studies will help you assess the feasibility and potential benefits of implementing similar technologies in your own training programs. This section should also include links to relevant journal articles and research papers exploring the efficacy of these technologies in emergency responder training.

Online learning platform providers: Several companies specialize in providing online learning platforms designed for fire service training. These platforms often offer a range of features, including interactive modules, assessment tools, and progress tracking capabilities. Researching and comparing different platform providers will help you identify a solution that best meets the specific needs of your organization and aligns with your budget. This section should also include a discussion of factors to consider when selecting an online learning platform, such as user-friendliness, functionality, and technical support.

III. Innovative Pedagogical Approaches:

This section focuses on the application of modern teaching methodologies to fire service training, emphasizing active learning, problem-based learning, and other strategies that promote deeper understanding and skill development.

Research articles on problem-based learning (PBL) in professional training: PBL is a student-centered approach where learners address complex, real-world problems. Extensive research demonstrates the effectiveness of PBL in developing critical thinking, problem-solving, and collaborative skills—all highly valuable assets for firefighters. Reviewing these studies will help you understand how to effectively integrate PBL into your training programs. This section should include a review of both the theoretical underpinnings of PBL and practical examples of its application in fire service training.

Case studies of successful implementations of active learning strategies in fire service training: This section should delve into specific instances where active learning has proven successful. Examples could include scenario-based training exercises, simulations, or role-playing activities that actively engage recruits and enhance their learning experience. These case studies will showcase the practical applications of active learning and offer insights into the strategies used to design and implement effective active learning programs.

IV. Leadership and Organizational Change:

This section addresses the crucial role of leadership in driving change and fostering a culture of innovation within fire service training departments.

Resources on organizational change management: Implementing new training methodologies often requires a shift in departmental culture and operational processes. Resources on organizational change management provide valuable insights into how to effectively navigate this process, address resistance to change, and build support for new initiatives. This should include strategies for communication, collaboration, and building consensus within the department. This section should also discuss the importance of effective leadership in driving and sustaining change within the organization.

Articles and case studies on successful leadership in fire service training: This section should showcase examples of successful fire service leaders who have successfully implemented innovative training programs. These case studies will provide valuable insights into the leadership strategies used to drive change, build support for new initiatives, and create a culture of continuous improvement within their organizations.

V. Continuous Professional Development for Instructors:

This section emphasizes the importance of ongoing learning and development for fire service training instructors, highlighting resources for enhancing their teaching skills and staying up-to-date with the latest training methodologies and technologies.

Professional development opportunities for fire service instructors: This section should list relevant professional organizations, conferences, and workshops that offer opportunities for fire service instructors to enhance their skills and knowledge. Examples could include the International Association of Fire Chiefs (IAFC) or the National Fire Academy (NFA). This section should also include information about online courses and webinars that provide training on effective teaching methodologies, the use of technology in training, and other relevant topics.

Resources on instructional design and technology: This section should provide links to websites and online resources that offer information on instructional design, including the selection, implementation and evaluation of training materials and programs. This section should also cover the integration of technology into the design process, which includes the use of learning management systems, virtual reality, and other technologies to enhance the effectiveness of fire service training.

This extensive list of resources provides a starting point for your own journey of continuous learning and improvement in fire service training. By embracing innovation and actively seeking out new knowledge, you can help shape the future of fire service training and equip the next generation of firefighters with the skills, knowledge, and resilience they need to excel in their demanding profession. Remember, the investment in training is an investment in the safety and well-being of your community.

The preceding sections have underscored the critical need for a paradigm shift in fire service training, moving beyond traditional methods to embrace a more engaging, effective, and technologically integrated approach. This evolution isn't simply about updating techniques; it's about fundamentally altering how we prepare future firefighters for the complex challenges they will face. The future of fire service training hinges on several key factors, all intrinsically linked to the role of the instructor.

Firstly, the increasing sophistication of firefighting technology demands a corresponding evolution in training methodologies. No longer can we rely solely on hands-on exercises and lectures; we must integrate simulation technology, virtual reality (VR), and augmented reality (AR) to create immersive and realistic training scenarios. VR and AR allow recruits to experience high-risk situations in a safe, controlled environment, practicing critical decision-making skills without the inherent dangers of real-world incidents. These technologies also offer the benefit of repeated practice and immediate feedback, fostering mastery of complex procedures and enhancing retention. The instructor's role here extends beyond simply operating the equipment; it's about designing effective virtual scenarios, interpreting the data generated by the simulations, and providing targeted feedback to individual trainees. This requires a deep understanding of both the technology and the pedagogical principles that underpin effective learning.

Furthermore, the future of fire service training necessitates a greater focus on personalized learning. Each recruit possesses unique learning styles, strengths, and weaknesses. Recognizing and catering to these individual differences is crucial for optimizing learning outcomes. Adaptive learning platforms, powered by artificial intelligence, are emerging as powerful tools that can personalize the learning experience. These platforms can assess a recruit's progress in real-time, adjusting the difficulty and content of training materials to match their individual needs. This allows for a more efficient and effective use of training time, ensuring that each recruit receives the support they need to reach their full potential. Instructors must become proficient in utilizing these platforms, understanding their capabilities, and interpreting the data they generate to inform their teaching strategies.

The incorporation of data-driven insights will play a significant role in shaping the future of fire service training. Through the use of learning analytics and performance tracking, instructors can gain a deeper understanding of individual recruit performance, identify areas of weakness, and tailor their instruction accordingly. This data-driven approach allows for continuous improvement and refinement of training programs, ensuring they remain relevant and effective. Instructors will need to become adept at interpreting this data, using it to inform their decisions, and adjusting their teaching strategies to optimize learning outcomes. Furthermore, this data can be used to assess the effectiveness of different training methodologies, allowing for evidence-based decision-making and ensuring that resources are allocated efficiently.

Another critical aspect of the future of fire service training is the fostering of a culture of continuous learning. Firefighting is a constantly evolving field, with new techniques, technologies, and hazards emerging regularly. To remain competent and effective, firefighters must embrace a lifelong commitment to professional development. The role of the instructor extends beyond initial recruit training; it encompasses the provision of ongoing support, mentorship, and access to professional development opportunities. This may include facilitating access to online learning resources, organizing workshops and seminars, and promoting participation in continuing education programs.

Moreover, the instructor's role is not limited to imparting knowledge and skills; it extends to fostering a strong sense of community and camaraderie within the fire service. Firefighting is a demanding and often dangerous profession, requiring strong teamwork and mutual support. The instructor has a crucial role in building a positive and supportive learning environment where recruits can develop strong relationships with their peers and instructors. This involves creating opportunities for collaborative
learning, encouraging teamwork, and fostering open communication. This collaborative environment is crucial in developing not just technically skilled firefighters, but well-rounded individuals capable of working effectively as part of a team.

In addition to these advancements, the future of fire service training will also need to address the changing demographics and diversity of the fire service itself. Training programs must be designed to be inclusive and accessible to individuals from all backgrounds, ensuring that all recruits receive the support they need to succeed. This may involve adapting training materials to accommodate different learning styles, providing language support, and addressing cultural sensitivities. Instructors must become culturally competent and sensitive, able to create an inclusive and welcoming learning environment for all recruits.

The challenges posed by climate change also demand a significant shift in fire service training. Increased frequency and intensity of wildfires, coupled with the impact of extreme weather events, require firefighters to possess specialized skills and knowledge. Training programs must incorporate these new realities, including training on wildfire suppression techniques, emergency response to climate-related disasters, and the specific hazards associated with these events. Instructors will need to stay abreast of the latest research and best practices in this area, ensuring that recruits are adequately prepared for these evolving challenges.

The integration of psychological resilience training is another critical aspect of the future of fire service training. Firefighters frequently face traumatic events and stressful situations, requiring strong psychological resilience to cope with the emotional and psychological demands of the job. Training programs must incorporate strategies for building resilience, including stress management techniques, mental health awareness, and peer support networks. Instructors play a critical role in this area, providing guidance, support, and promoting a culture of mental wellness within the fire service.

Finally, the future of fire service training depends on the ongoing professional development of instructors themselves. As the field of firefighting evolves, so too must the skills and knowledge of those who train the next generation of firefighters. Instructors must continuously seek out professional development opportunities, attending conferences, participating in workshops, and engaging in ongoing learning to stay abreast of the latest training methodologies, technologies, and best practices. This commitment to continuous professional development will ensure that the fire service training remains relevant, effective, and capable of meeting the evolving needs of the profession. Investing in instructors' professional development is an investment in the future of the fire service.

The future of fire service training is bright, filled with potential for innovation and improvement. However, this potential can only be realized through a concerted effort to adapt, innovate, and invest in the training process. The role of the instructor in this transformation is paramount. They are not merely instructors; they are mentors, leaders, and innovators, shaping the future of fire service safety and preparedness. By embracing new technologies, pedagogical approaches, and a commitment to continuous learning, instructors can equip the next generation of firefighters with the skills, knowledge, and resilience they need to excel in this demanding and vital profession. The investment in effective fire service training is, ultimately, an investment in the safety and well-being of our communities.

Back Matter

First and foremost, I want to express my sincere gratitude to the countless firefighters I've had the privilege of training throughout my career. Your dedication, resilience, and commitment to service have been my constant inspiration. This book is as much a testament to your unwavering spirit as it is to the evolution of fire service training.

Special thanks are due to the instructors and training officers who have shared their wisdom and expertise with me over the years. Your insights and experiences have shaped my understanding of effective pedagogical practices and profoundly influenced the content of this book. Your collaborative spirit and commitment to continuous improvement within the fire service are truly commendable. Capt. Burns and Chief Strickland, thank you for all of the years of mentoring and supporting me.

I also want to acknowledge the unwavering support of my wife April, and my girls Ashley, Madison, and Lillian who have patiently endured late nights and countless hours of writing. Your understanding and encouragement have been invaluable throughout this project, I love you so very much.

Made in the USA
Columbia, SC
10 June 2025